Finding the Joy in
TEACHING

Finding the Joy in
TEACHING

From the Toilet to the
Scaled Universe

Melissa Fredericks

gatekeeper press

Columbus, Ohio

Finding the Joy in Teaching: From the Toilet to the Scaled Universe

Published by Gatekeeper Press
2167 Stringtown Rd, Suite 109
Columbus, OH 43123-2989
www.GatekeeperPress.com

The cover design, interior formatting, typesetting, and editorial work for this book are entirely the product of the author. Gatekeeper Press did not participate in and is not responsible for any aspect of these elements.

Library of Congress Control Number: 2020939330

ISBN (paperback): 9781662901553
eISBN: 9781662901546

I dedicate this book to any teacher or person who has ever found joy in
something unexpected, unusual, or even annoying.
I hope to meet you someday and hear your crazy stories.

I also dedicate this book to those of you who haven't yet found joy in such situations.
May the stories in this book inspire you to
view your next hassle a little differently.

Table of Contents

Preface
Finding the Joy

Early in my teaching life, a veteran educator gave me some of the best advice of my career to date. These may not have been her exact words, but this was the sentiment:

> "Whatever you do, whatever happens, however hard the day is, however frustrated you are by a kid, parent, colleague or administrator, always remember to find the joy."

As a young person, still in my twenties, I smiled and said something like,

> "Of course! I love being a teacher. It's amazing! The world is rainbows and unicorns. Isn't it great that I make a difference and aren't kids cute?"

Years later, I am concluding my twenty-first year as a teacher. I've taught...

- Preschool in a high-poverty neighborhood
- Life skills to middle-school students with emotional disabilities

- K–4 in a highly successful, high-performing charter school with mainly middle-class students
- High school special education; including self-contained, resource room, and consult, in a large urban, high-poverty school

I've seen a lot over the years! I've had days when the sky was void of rainbows and was instead dark and stormy. Rather than finding myself in a field of unicorns, at times, I have experienced a teaching world filled with more vicious, ferocious animals. And I learned a long time ago that kids are not always that cute. But even after all these years, I can honestly say that I love being a teacher.

With all of the media coverage of the difficult conditions teachers face, many people find it surprising that I love my job so much. News sources report that teacher education enrollment has declined in recent years and that many teachers never make it to their 5-year "teachiversary." Our nation is facing a shortage in one of the most important and needed workforces and the reasons are many. Every day, teachers encounter students with emotional, academic, and social needs that can be overwhelming. They deal with lack of adequate resources and planning time, as well as pressure from multiple sources including parents, school districts, and states. I too experience these unfortunate realities on a daily basis.

Some days, I go home mentally and physically exhausted and wonder if I have it in me to make it through another day. But thankfully, most days, despite the challenges, I feel satisfied and rewarded and good about the seven hours I spent in my home away from home with my school family.

The key to my longevity and happiness is that somewhere along the way, I figured out how to find the joy in teaching, despite, and often because of, all of the craziness involved in being a teacher.

Finding the joy isn't easy. It involves being willing to work hard, persevere, maintain a positive attitude, be open-minded, and possess a wicked good sense of humor. To find the joy, you must look for it and be willing to accept it in some pretty weird places. Teaching is hardly ever what I expect it to be, so I've come to terms with the fact that I might find my next dose of joy in a bag of rabbit poop or on the wing of a dead honeybee.

It's time to put the message out. Yes, teaching is difficult and the conditions are often not ideal. However, teaching can also be one of the most amazing journeys a person can take. My hope is that this book helps teachers embrace the unexpected and find joy in it. By reading this book, I believe you will be able to set aside worries, at least for a few moments, and find the joy in teaching.

I've found the joy in teaching everywhere from an overflowing toilet to a colorful, confusing economics board game. As you read this book, I anticipate that you will laugh, be shocked, and even experience some sadness or anger. Most importantly, I hope you will come to understand that the joy of teaching is in the short stories that make up the big picture and what you do to embrace each moment.

Introduction

Find the Joy One Story at a Time

Every teacher has stories. Lots of them! On a daily basis, students are funny, amazing, annoying, and heartbreaking, all within a seven-hour period. While students are being their unpredictable selves, lessons either thrive, survive or fail miserably. Some kids learn material immediately, while others need more time. Some students are good to each other and themselves and some are downright rotten. In a single day, any number of things can happen: failed technology, administration visits, parent encounters, reports due. At the end of 420 minutes, every teacher goes home with a handful of new stories to muse over.

Teaching is made up of stories, and so, that is how I've organized this book. There are four parts to *Finding the Joy in Teaching:*

- Embracing Curriculum: Finding Joy in Topics Meant to Be
- Strengthening Assignments: Finding Joy in Student-Driven Projects and Activities
- Enhancing Classroom Management: Finding Joy in Creating a Positive Environment
- Developing Relationships with the Students: Finding Joy in the Best Part of All

Each part begins with an overview of that aspect of teaching and what can make it difficult. Following each introduction, there are 4–6 true stories from my life as a teacher. Everything in this book actually happened. I've changed names and tried to avoid revealing locations or years in which things happened. Other than that, if it's in this book, it's true. Get ready to read about an overflowing toilet, a senior who needs constant pep-talks to go to class, a group of out-of-control four-year-olds, and other calamities turned into triumph.

The stories will make you laugh out loud, drop your jaw in disbelief, and maybe even cry. You will feel relief in knowing you are not the only one who has encountered craziness in the classroom. Most importantly, each story will help you find the joy in teaching as you muck through the challenges. The stories are not in the order in which they occurred; they are divided into the four parts of the book and document times when I have found joy in topics meant to be, kid projects and activities, classroom management, and relationships with kids.

After each story, I've included a list of three actions that a teacher can do to find joy in similar situations. So, after you savor my joyful story, you essentially have an action plan for finding joy in your own daily stories. Following the list of three actions, I've included a writing/thinking exercise you can do to help you consciously find joy in teaching. The exercises are not elaborate or lengthy because, let's face it, teachers don't have a ton of extra time for "exercises!" They are meant to engage your brain in a different way than you might usually and help you find joy in teaching in a place you never expected.

At the end of the book, I give some final remarks on spreading the joy. I don't promise that this book will solve all that ails you as a teacher, however, I do hope that by the time you get to the end, you will be harnessing the joy in teaching and telling your stories to anyone who will listen.

Embracing Curriculum:
Finding Joy in Topics Meant to Be

The pressure to meet educational standards and get students to "pass the test" is immense. Many of the teachers I know feel overwhelmed by the task of bringing all students to a prescribed level of achievement without regard for differences in developmental levels or environmental situations. Schools and communities adopt curriculum with the intended goal of aiding teachers in helping kids achieve, but in many cases, the curriculum and imposed standards cause more stress on teachers, students, parents, and stakeholders.

Somewhere along the way, the wonder of childhood has been lost to text-coded paragraphs, abstract equations, and formulaic essays. At the same time, the drive in teachers to be creative while sharing their passions with students has taken a backseat to the stress they feel for each upcoming evaluation. It doesn't have to be this way!

In this section of the book, you will learn how to embrace the curriculum and bring back the wonder, passion, and creativity for yourself and your students.

In most cases, depending on where you teach, you have at least some flexibility to meet the standards in ways that are engaging and student-centered. Some of you may teach in a place that allows you freedom in planning units and experiences as long as the standards are aligned. In other places, perhaps the only flexibility you have is to read a good book to your students every so often.

Wherever you are, I hope you will see that embracing unusual topics as much as possible can drive your instruction and allow you and your students to find the joy in the curriculum. In addition, using bizarre and surprising topics can lead to students achieving at a higher level than expected and surpassing the standards. Get ready to learn how I found joy in the toilet, cardboard towns, rabbit poop and dog footprints, and a gecko named Raptor.

The crazy topics that ignited joy in my teaching life probably won't be the same for you. However, don't worry! The Practical Applications section after each story will help you find the joy in similar situations, and the writing/thinking exercises will give you even more ideas for how to liven up your curriculum in unconventional ways.

The Toilet

One year, my co-teacher and I had a general education first-grade class that seemed somewhat unfamiliar with the toilet and, consequently, completely fascinated by it. Of course, I know that the children weren't really new to using a toilet, but at times it seemed like it. Until we had the great idea (you'll read about it soon) that changed our frustrations into joy, we had all kinds of trouble with that porcelain seat in the small room at the back of our classroom.

First of all, the kids wouldn't flush. Okay, lots of kids do that, but most of them don't leave their treasures in there so that they can show their friends...or their teachers! One boy called me into the bathroom one day. Thinking there was some kind of problem, I went in with him, leaving the door ajar behind me. I had been duped. There was no problem; well, at least not the type I was expecting. He simply wanted to show me that his poop looked like chicken nuggets. What followed that afternoon was a somewhat awkward call to his parents.

The kids also really liked toilet paper. I mean, they *really* liked it. I don't remember the school buying special toilet paper that year, but the kids must have thought differently. One day, a boy came out of the bathroom and said, "I didn't do it." Before my co-teacher could ask exactly

3

what he didn't do, one of the biggest floods I have ever seen came pouring out from under the bathroom door.

As my co-teacher and the TA frantically tried to roll up the rug, I scurried the class, many of whom were screaming, to the other side of the room and called the office who alerted the janitors. After the newly formed lake was sucked up from our classroom, my co-teacher and I had a meeting with the class. My co-teacher, who was and still is one of the most amazing teachers/human beings on the planet, carefully discussed with the children how much toilet paper is necessary to use for different bathroom experiences and what to do if something goes wrong in the bathroom.

When the kids weren't flooding the bathroom or leaving their special treasures floating, they thought it was fun to experiment by putting other objects in the toilet. We fished out all kinds of toys ranging from solitary legos to pretty dolls who should have been sitting at their miniature tables drinking tiny cups of imaginary tea rather than bathing in pools of bacteria-filled water. One day, someone put an uncapped blue marker in the toilet. That was really cool because it turned the water blue!

I never realized that nearly an entire class of six-year-olds could fit inside a room that was only about 25 square feet, but the day of the blue toilet water proved to my co-teacher and me that these kids would do anything to see something cool in the bathroom. After school, soon after the blue water day, my co-teacher, the teaching assistant and I discussed what to do about this class's obsession with the bathroom. We realized that if we couldn't beat them, we should join them. If they thought the bathroom was that amazing, then who were we to take that away from them! We hatched our plan.

As luck would have it, at the progressive charter school where we worked, it was time to start planning our next unit of study. The school had a loose framework for the curriculum that was based on state standards. Our task for the next 3 months was to teach the students about how a city works. Among the many subjects suggested for us to focus our instruction on was City Infrastructure. Included in City Infrastructure was electricity, water treatment, fire and police, roads and bridges, and sewage treatment. Sewage treatment! We decided that our launch for the next unit would be...the amazing toilet!

I'll never forget the day we launched that unit! We told the kids that since they loved putting things in the toilet so much, we were going to study where all of that stuff went. What happens to a blue marker or chicken nugget-shaped poop when you flush? As we looked at their shocked faces and ignored the puzzled looks, we proceeded to teach them a song about the toilet and show a video with a gecko narrator who gave us a tour of the waste treatment plant.

The next week we visited the sewage treatment plant and had a tour. Our guides excitedly walked us through each step of sewage treatment. The first stop was the screening station where big items like toys, garbage, and once an alligator are caught! These things have to be taken out before the water can be cleaned. We talented teachers then facilitated an "ah-ha" moment for the students. Foreign objects should not be flushed down the toilet because it makes the process of cleaning the water one step harder.

On that tour, we also got to see and smell the waste being separated into parts, skimmed, anaerobically digested, spun, and chlorinated. Gross, but memorable and, honestly, really cool!

Back at school, we made diagrams of sewage treatment, wrote stories, and read books. We focused on sewage treatment for a few weeks before branching out to other areas of city infrastructure including electricity, roads and bridges, fire and police, and water treatment. By the end of our three-month focus on city infrastructure, our first-graders had a fairly sophisticated understanding of the services and facilities needed in a city.

It makes me laugh that such an engaging unit started with a flooded toilet! It almost seems metaphorical; the joy of teaching will come to you when you're wading through toilet water. We found the joy in teaching in two important ways as a result of this experience. First of all, the kids eventually started using the bathroom more appropriately. Not having to fish things out of the toilet was a small victory for us. More important than the proper bathroom behavior that resulted from this unit, was the excitement the kids had about what we were studying. We hit the standards, covered the curriculum, and had a good time, all because of our classroom toilet!

You too can find joy in the toilet.

---

1. Keep calm and maintain a sense of humor when kids do things that are developmentally typical but are nevertheless annoying, such as exhibiting a fascination with bathroom stuff.

2. Be as emergent as possible with your curriculum. Observe your students and listen to them to learn what they are interested in, then infuse those ideas to the extent allowed at your setting. Even if you can't stray too far from what the school dictates, hopefully you can at least read a book aloud that acknowledges your students' interests.

3. Take students to cool and unexpected places, like a smelly sewage treatment plant. If you are lucky enough to have a field trip budget, plan for trips that deepen the students' understanding of the topic they are studying. If you don't have a budget, try fundraising so your students can experience at least one field trip a year. If all else fails, use the internet and your imagination to take them on virtual field trips.

Writing/Thinking Exercise

Describe an annoying or disgusting habit that your class has.

_____

_____

_____

_____

Now list at least 5 ways that you could use that annoying or disgusting habit as a way to teach them something really cool.

1. _____

2. _____

3. _____

4. _____

5. _____

Cardboard Towns

As a second-year teacher, I landed a job as a Middle School Life Skills teacher. The job was located about an hour from where I lived and was part of a local BOCES. At the time, I was also in graduate school in an Early Childhood program. It seems crazy to me now that I took that job when it was such a long commute and I was going to school in the evenings focusing on a completely different age level! I guess being young meant I was also full of energy!

As a conscientious young person eager to get a good start, I asked my principal if I could come in early to set up. I remember walking into the classroom and there was one table in the room. That was it! The principal showed me the room and said, "We need to get you some furniture." As I've learned over the years, in teaching and in life, sometimes a blank slate is the best gift. When you start with next to nothing, almost anything you do is going to improve the situation.

In the next few weeks before school started, things sort of came together. The principal showed me the storeroom, which had spare consumable materials, and told me I could take what I needed. The janitor found me some basic furniture, so everyone had a place to sit on the first day. The teacher next door, who taught the same type of class just with older students, gave me some resources on what I should teach students in a life skills class. I also gathered up the few materials I had collected during my student teaching and first year as a teacher. On the first day, the classroom had slightly more than just a table. We didn't start with a lot, but we had enough.

I honestly don't remember the first day with students. I'm sure I was excited but a little overwhelmed since that is how the first day is for me every year. I do remember that as time went on, I really started to enjoy that job. The students and TA and I developed a strong rapport from the start. I recall the social worker saying to me early on, "You seem to really know your students."

I also enjoyed the curriculum, which was very open-ended. Basically, as long as I was teaching them reading, writing, and math at their levels and life skills such as cooking, shopping, money management, career exploration, and decision making, I could design the program in any way I thought was best. By the third year in the position (which was my last year there, since that year I gave birth to my oldest daughter and decided to look for something closer to home), I had developed a pretty amazing way of teaching the life skills curriculum.

Remember that table? Well, we covered it with white paper and drew some roads on it. Then everyone got a cardboard box apartment to put in the town. Except that first, they had to get jobs. I brought in applications from fast food and retail places and, as part of our reading and writing instruction, students filled them out. Then they had to interview for the job. This helped them work on speaking and listening as well as the actual skill of interviewing. Plus, it was great fun. I was the supervisor of course! I even managed to find a visor and made a name pin so that I could play the part.

Once everyone got a job, they started getting paid (in monopoly type money), then they could finally pay for the first month's rent on their cardboard apartment. At this point, everyone had pretend jobs with pretend paychecks. They had checkbooks they had to keep balanced, which we worked on during our math instruction. The table was covered in white paper with roads drawn and empty shoeboxes. People around us started to wonder what was going on!

Let me take a step back and tell you a little more about the school. It was a middle and high school, and the classes were all 6:1:1's consisting of six students, one teacher, and one teaching assistant. The students were all classified as Emotionally Disabled and this was a pretty restrictive environment. Most of them had been in less restrictive placements that didn't work out, so they landed at this school. Some had been in more severe places, such as residential, and had come back to the community.

There were always a lot of behavior issues throughout the school such as swearing, spitting, flipping over furniture, hitting, kicking, and non-compliance. My room was no different. Even though I had a good relationship with them, especially by the third year since I had most of them all three years, they still displayed the types of behaviors that were typical of kids with emotional disabilities. Plus, my students all had intellectual disabilities as well. The teachers in the school were great, but no one else had ever thought of making a cardboard town with their students and using it to teach the curriculum!

Attempting to engage in what turned out to be a project that ended up lasting about 4 months with the type of students I had in that class was probably a little nuts.

But I did it. Like I said, I was young and energetic. And that project turned out to be amazing! I've told you the first few parts of the project already. Since this story isn't so much about the actual project content but more about the lessons learned in finding joy, I'll give you an overview of the rest.

Once they had their empty apartments, they "bought" furniture from magazines with the money in their pretend checking accounts. I brought in a cash register and more play money and we worked on money skills throughout the project whenever anyone had to "buy" anything. They practiced their money skills going grocery shopping, buying holiday gifts, and buying new clothes.

They also learned about public transportation, cooking, cleaning, going out to eat, and emergency and safety skills. With each new skill or content, we simulated the activity in the cardboard town, as well as reading about it and practicing it through hands-on activities. In addition, the students learned about important parts of a community such as hospitals, fire departments, post offices, schools, etc and added those places to our cardboard town. When all was said and done, we had a cardboard town that was quite special!

In all seriousness, though, the cardboard town was special to the students. Throughout the 4 months we had it up in our classroom, the students had many behavioral outbursts. We had expectations and a behavior management system, but behavior problems still occurred on a daily basis. That was why they were placed in the type of setting they were in. The room was trashed more than once. But no one ever touched the cardboard town.

I can only theorize that they must have felt proud of all of the work they put into the cardboard town. The fact that these young teenagers, who had emotional and intellectual disabilities, felt respect for themselves and their classmates because of a table covered in cut-out pictures and cardboard boxes gives me such joy! It reminds me that to be a good teacher, you don't need all of the fanciest gadgets and resources. Those can definitely help and I have nothing against them, but they are not the most important parts of teaching.

The three most important things are to make sure you know your students well, develop a productive learning community, and approach whatever curriculum you are slated to teach with knowledge, enthusiasm, and creativity. If you do those three things, your students will learn what they need to know, even when you have little more than a table and some shoeboxes to work with.

You too can find joy in cardboard towns.

1. Do the best you can with what you have. When resources are not plentiful, use your imagination and you'll likely come up with something brilliant.
2. Gather items from the community to enhance your lessons and create authenticity. If you are teaching students in a life skills program how to look for a job, bring in the classified ads. If you are teaching a general education third-grade class about elapsed time, bring in bus schedules. Whatever the topic or level is, the more connections that students can make to the "real world," the more they will understand that what they learn in school applies to their everyday lives.

3. Save recyclables! You never know what great idea you might have for toilet paper rolls, cereal boxes, foam peanuts, and of course, shoeboxes.

Writing/Thinking Exercise

Take a trip to your local mall. Collect anything that is free; brochures, bus schedules, restaurant menus, etc. List at least 5 of the items below and describe one way you could use each of them in the classroom.

1. _____

_____

2. _____

_____

3. _____

_____

4. _____

_____

5. _____

_____

6. _____

_____

7. _____

_____

8. _____

_____

9. _____

_____

10. _____

_____

Things You Find on the Playground: Rabbit Poop and Dog Footprints

"Ms. F., Ms. F., we found something!"

I followed a few of my first-graders as they excitedly took me past the see-saw and climbing wall, dodging swarms of kids in the process. I found myself looking at the treasure they had found on the playground: a pile of rabbit poop.

"What do you think it is?" I asked.

"Poop!" they shouted in unison.

"Who do you think pooped on our playground?" I asked.

"I don't know, some kind of animal," one of them said.

"What should we do?" I asked.

"We have to find out what animal did this!"

"Good idea," I said.

Then, I went inside and got a plastic baggie and a pair of gloves. I donned the gloves, put the mystery poop in the baggie, and blew the whistle for the students to get in line and come inside.

Different year...different kids...different discovery...same story...

"Ms. F., Ms. F., come, we found something!"

I followed my students past the spinners and the playhouse to the muddy section of the playground near the climber. There, on the ground, were the distinct footprints of a dog.

"What do you think it is?" I asked.

"Footprints!" they shouted in unison.

"Whose footprints do you think are on our playground?" I asked.

"I don't know, some kind of animal," one of them said.

"What should we do?" I asked.

"We have to find out what animal did this!"

"Good idea," I said.

Then, I went inside and got the camera so I could take a picture of the prints. After that, I blew the whistle for the students to get in line and come inside.

You might think that playground time is mostly part of the elementary school day so that the teachers can have a breather; 20 minutes to stand and talk to a colleague while keeping half an eye on the students. Perhaps you have a more advanced philosophy and understand that at least 20 minutes of daily exercise and fresh air are crucial to a child's brain development. Maybe you even realize that the social negotiations and physical risk-taking that occur on the playground are important parts of childhood.

Whatever your stance on recess, I bet you didn't know that the treasure kids find on the playground of a school located in an urban area, such as a pile of rabbit poop or dog footprints, can lead the class on three-month inquiries about animals and habitats. But that is what happened two separate years, while teaching with a different co-teacher each time.

After the rabbit waste had been collected, the class sat in a circle around the edge of our carpet and we passed the bag around to examine its contents. Over the next couple of days, students looked at pictures of poop in books and identification charts to try to figure out what type of animal had been on our playground. They narrowed the possibilities to squirrel, deer, and rabbit.

Then one day, one of the little girls in the class brought something in from home to show everyone. It was a plastic baggie filled with her pet rabbit's droppings! Now remember, the class had been talking about poop and looking at pictures of it for three days. Never once in those three days had this girl mentioned that she had a pet rabbit and that its poop looked like the scat we had found on the playground. When she brought in the baggie, I couldn't help but wonder when she had the "ah-ha" moment that helped her realize she had important information to share with the class.

In any case, when Jada brought in her pet's waste, we called for all students to gather around the edge of the carpet and once again, we passed a bag of poop around to be examined. How exciting! We had found a match and solved a mystery! A rabbit had been hopping around our playground and gone to the bathroom. This discovery, and some preplanned coaxing from my co-teacher and I, inspired the class to wonder what other animals lived in the area and possibly used the playground when we weren't around.

For the next two months, the class spent time looking for animals in the field behind our school, on the playground, in the neighborhood surrounding the school, in their backyards, and in the local parks. They studied whatever animals they found outdoors back in the classroom through books, videos, and photos.

Similarly, after the dog footprints had been photographed, we sat the class down around the edge of the carpet and examined the picture. At first, most students thought the prints were from a dog's foot. Then, one of the first-graders suggested that maybe a bear had been walking around our playground, and they began to wonder if bears or other animals lived in the neighborhood and went on the playground when we weren't looking. The next day, my co-teacher and I presented the class with books about animals and footprints. The students discovered that different types of animals had different footprints.

As a class, we identified 3 things to look at as we explored footprints: size, shape, and number of toes. We were happy to realize that the animal on the playground couldn't be a bear because their print has five toes and a dog print only has four toes. Students also quickly eliminated the deer, since its print is two long toes with small dots behind them. One little girl brought in a book from the library about Bigfoot. She was convinced that sasquatch had been on our playground until we determined that the size and shape didn't match the print we had found. Phew!

Finally, after a few days of research, the class narrowed down the possibilities to tiger, coyote, dog, and cougar. In Math, we were learning about taking data, sorting it, and representing it, so we decided that the entire class (30 kids and 3 teachers) would go out into the neighborhood with surveys on clipboards, explain our mystery to nice people out for a walk, and ask them if they had ever seen a tiger, coyote, dog or cougar around our school. We got a few strange looks, to say the least! Most people played along though, and we discovered that dog sightings were very common in the neighborhood. We even saw a few dogs!

When we got back to the class and organized the data, we were positive that the mystery footprint leaver on our playground was a dog. We spent the next two months studying other animals that we had been interested in while reading about footprints. We tried to focus on local animals and spent time looking for those animals in the field behind our school, on the playground, in the neighborhood surrounding the school, in our backyards, and in the local parks.

Different years...different kids...different discoveries...same joy...

As a teacher, you have so much curriculum and content to cover. The years of the rabbit poop and dog footprints were no different. Our schoolwide curriculum map dictated that we teach about local animals and habitats. The common core state standards guided our work in ELA and Math. The joy in this story is that we covered all of that and more by latching on to something that the students had discovered and were interested in.

If we had dismissed their findings as trivial or gross, we would have lost the opportunity to deliver the curriculum in a way that highlighted the natural curiosity and enthusiasm of six-year-olds. I am so thankful that during the years I worked at the charter school, I had the excellent fortune to work with other adults who knew how important it was to foster emergent learning opportunities for students, even when it meant passing a bag of poop around the class or asking ridiculous questions to grown-ups out for a morning walk.

You too can find joy in things you find on the playground.

1. Play dumb. If your students are curious about something, instead of giving them all of the information, let them discover the answers for themselves. Let them ask questions, research, communicate, and explore, even when the inquiry seems to have an obvious answer.
2. Don't be afraid of gross stuff. Some of the most important scientific discoveries over the past 200 years, blood circulation, pasteurization, and penicillin to name a few, have involved disgusting processes and fluids.
3. Incorporate student ideas and inquiries as much as possible into your curriculum by studying the standards closely in order to understand what skills and content you are supposed to cover. Once you have a clear understanding of the standards, you'll realize that they give you freedom rather than limit you because you will be able to envision and create multiple ways to help kids meet the standards, perhaps even by using rabbit poop or dog footprints as a gateway to learning.

Writing/Thinking Exercise

Go for a walk and make an effort to notice things that you normally pass by. Write a list of at least 5 things you think your students would find interesting.

1. _____

_____

2. _____

_____

3. _____

_____

4. _____

_____

5. _____

_____

A Gecko Named Raptor

Over the years, I have had many classroom pets, Bear the hamster, Hoppy Swim the frog, Nemo the fish, Raptor the gecko, and a slew of unnamed pets, including a hermit crab, a millipede, and even an anemone. All of these pets fostered responsibility in my students by engaging them in tasks such as feeding and cage maintenance and provided hours of entertainment with their crazy animal shenanigans. And as with everything in this book, these pets give me stories to tell.

I remember clearly the time that a rather rambunctious first-grader stuck his hand in the hermit crab tank. It bit him of course. The boy, in response to the pain and shock of being bitten by a hermit crab, flung the crustacean across the room. Another child alerted me to the problem. When I asked Darren, the hermit crab flinger, where our pet was now, he said, "I don't know where that junk is. That junk bit me." To this, I said, "Well, we need to find that junk so let's start looking."

Luckily the hermit crab had not been thrown too far and I was able to return him to his heated wood chip and coconut hut abode. The frog I had with a different class, Hoppy Swim, also got out one day and we never did find him. Kids searched under tables and chairs, in the closets, in the bathroom and all around, but he was just gone. We had a memorial service without the body.

All of my classroom pets have been memorable, but none have ever had the same effect on a class as Raptor the gecko. He became the subject of the best teaching unit my co-teacher, TA, and I ever wrote and delivered. This is the story of a lizard who went on a big imaginary adventure and taught the Kindergarteners about local habitats and animals.

I don't recall exactly how the idea for the "Where in the World Is Raptor the Gecko?" teaching unit was hatched. At the charter school, we taught 3-month units or "learning expeditions," which were planned by us teachers. There was a school curriculum framework based on state standards that we had to adhere to, but the way we taught the curriculum was open-ended. "Outside of the box" ideas were welcome. This unit was 'outside of the box' figuratively and literally; the box being Raptor the gecko's cage.

On the day the plan was concocted, my co-teacher, TA, and I were sitting around our Kindergarten-sized table in tiny chairs during our professional development planning day. Our task was to design a 3-month unit that would engage the students and teach them about local habitats and animals. At this point, we had taught together for several years and had covered this curriculum with previous classes.

The other years we taught the curriculum, we had planned great learning expeditions that we could have easily repeated. One year, we even rewrote the story of the Lorax, and kids made costumes and acted it out. We could have pulled out that old plan and repeated it with this new group of kids. But we didn't. Because one of us had the idea to center the entire unit around our class pet going on a fictional 3-month journey.

In the days leading up to the official launch of "Where in the World Is Raptor the Gecko?" some odd things happened. Raptor's water dish was empty one day. Another time, he was out of food. Then, we found wadded up paper towels in his cage. We teachers made a big fuss about these occurrences with the class, stressing how important it was to properly take care of Raptor.

In reality of course, we were the ones messing with the tank. The kids listened, but as 5-year-olds do. They weren't too concerned about poor old Raptor. The day after the garbage in the tank, Raptor's cage was empty (he was being secretly held in a different cage at my house) and there was a note inside. It said something like,

"Dear friends,

I love you all dearly, but I am not happy with my home. There wasn't enough food one day and I was thirsty another day. Then, I found garbage where I sleep. That was the last straw. I am leaving to explore local habitats and find a new home.

Sincerely,
Raptor"

We read the note aloud very seriously to the class during our morning meeting. The kid sitting next to my co-teacher put his hands on his face like Macaulay Culkin in the movie *Home Alone* and fell over. Most of the 5-year-olds just stared. One student marveled at the idea that Raptor could write and wondered how he held a pencil with his little arms.

(Now, if you are reading this and thinking, "I can't believe they lied to a bunch of kindergarteners! What a mean trick," think about the millions of parents and adults over the years who have convinced small children that their teeth are picked up by a fairy who delivers money, eggs are hidden in the Spring by a giant bunny, and a fat man in a red suit flies in a sleigh led by reindeer, trespasses into houses, and drops off presents.)

Although we did feel a little guilty about our non-truth, we knew that the kids would be so engaged in looking for Raptor in the local habitats that the reading, writing, and learning opportunities were a sufficient trade-off. We also agreed that if anyone got really upset or it seemed the unit was turning sour, we would just change our plans.

After the initial letter from Raptor, the students wrote a letter back to him and pleaded for him to come home promising a clean cage and ample food and water. We left the letters for Raptor and hoped for the best. The next day, there was no lizard in the tank, but there was a new letter. Our precious pet had written us to tell us that he stopped by and got our letters. He was going out to explore the habitat in the field adjacent to our school. We donned our coats and headed outside.

We observed many animals; squirrels, birds, ants, caterpillars, etc, but no gecko. When we came back to the classroom, we discovered that by a lucky coincidence, we had just the right books for the research we needed to do! Students read about fields and animals who live there and found out a few alarming pieces of information. For one thing, geckos cannot live in fields. It is not warm enough and there aren't enough places to hide. Furthermore, birds EAT lizards! We had to warn Raptor before he became bird food! So, the students wrote their next letters to the reptile on the loose and anxiously awaited his response.

You can probably guess what happened next and after that and after that. That's right. We engaged in a cycle of events with our class pet. First he'd write to us about a habitat he wanted to explore. Then we would visit that habitat and research it, and find out that geckos couldn't live there. We would send warning letters and wait for him to start the cycle over with his next letter about the habitat he was going to visit next.

It sounds ridiculous, right? Well, it was slightly absurd, however, it was also incredibly powerful. Throughout the 3-month learning expedition, students were passionate about their research and writing. The goal of finding Raptor and bringing him home gave their work purpose and they took it very seriously. They cared about him and wanted him safe and sound at home.

Eventually, the 5-year-olds, guided by their mildly insane teachers, researched how to create a natural habitat for a gecko. I bought a 40-gallon tank on Craigslist. When I went to pick it up, I told the seller about the project. He volunteered to come in to the class and help us set up a natural habitat for Raptor. So, a week later, in came my new friend to help the eager Kindergarteners set up a luxury home that would help bring home the pet they missed dearly. It worked of course!

Before long, Raptor magically appeared back in the classroom. The excitement and pride were beyond measure the next day when we discovered that Raptor was snug in his heated home complete with Malaysian driftwood, a drainage system, and live-rooted and air plants. We sang songs and read books to our beloved gecko to celebrate his return.

The joy you feel when you realize that a group of five-year-olds has defied the developmentally appropriate norm of being egocentric and stepped away from themselves to care for another living creature is immense. It means that as a teacher, you've done something to help raise citizens who think about and help others. If you can achieve that by concocting a story about an adventurous gecko or some other crazy thing, then I say go for it!

You too can find joy in a gecko named Raptor (or a different pet by another name)...

1. Get a classroom pet. Classroom pets encourage responsibility, foster empathy, provide comfort, and are entertaining. They are an authentic way to teach children about habitats and animals around the world. They provide opportunities for reading and writing. They give students something to care about.
2. Have a little fun with your lessons. Use your imagination and create activities that will engage students and make them wonder.
3. Bring kids outside and let them observe animals, plants, and nature. Even if you can only get out to the playground or a grassy area by the school, dig a hole and look for life. If there is no place for your students to observe the natural world, then show them really good nature videos and have them imagine they are in that place.

Writing/Thinking Exercise

Imagine life from your pet's point of view. Write a letter to yourself, your class, your family or a friend from your pet.

_____

_____

_____

_____

_____

_____

_____

_____

_____

_____

_____

Holiday Debate

Caleb's big brown eyes looked up at the 6 foot, 2 inches, well-dressed lawyer sitting at the table across from him, put down his last "talking chip," and said in a sturdy voice,

"But I still think that we should celebrate Indigenous Peoples' Day instead of Columbus Day."

He went on to explain his reasons with conviction, drawing on what he had learned about the importance of bringing awareness to the history of Native people in our country and the trauma they experienced as a result of European contact in the Americas. I should mention that Caleb, at the time, was in the third grade.

I should also mention, before this story goes any further, that it is not my intention to present my own stance in the debate over whether on the second Monday of each October we should celebrate Columbus Day or Indigenous Peoples' Day. This story is about the joy that ensued from the teaching unit on Native Americans that lead to the debate between little Caleb, an adorable 8-year-old; small for his age with a great set of dimples, and Mr. G., a well-known professional in our city who happened to be the father of one of our other students.

At the charter school, where I worked for 15 years, like most other elementary schools, teachers were expected to teach about Native Americans. The charter school was progressive, and I felt fortunate that we as staff were provided with professional development on Native Americans. We had a connection with the local Native American historical site located about half an hour from our school, and we were located on the campus of a science museum that had Native American exhibits and artifacts.

The local Native American historical site was located where the largest Seneca village of the 17th century once was. There was a replica longhouse there with artifacts and hiking trails and Seneca people who worked at the site. At the science museum on our campus, there were large dioramas that showcased the lives of people in Native villages in different regions of the United States from the 1600s to the 1800s. As staff, we were lucky enough to be able to learn from Seneca people about their culture and had access to lots of accurate information about Native people.

Our students were lucky too! They also benefited from the connections we had with the local historic site and the science museum. At the time that I taught the unit that lead to the dispute between Caleb and Mr. G., I had already covered the Native American curriculum at the charter school six times with Kindergarten or first-graders. Despite the abundant resources we had available to us, I always struggled with teaching the unit on Native Americans.

As an adult, I realize that as a child, much of the Native American history I learned, especially from the time period spanning from European contact to the Western expansion, was inaccurate or incomplete. Although I subsequently learned a lot at the charter school on the subject, I still worried about teaching something incorrectly.

Another challenge was that the children, even as young as Kindergarten and first grade, already had some misconceptions about Native Americans from books or movies they had seen that stereotypically portrayed the culture. I remember one young artist whose favorite thing to draw and write about in first grade was "cowboys and Indians." Belief systems are hard to change in adults and young children.

In addition to their misconceptions about Native Americans, many of the children I had in the classes I taught prior to this story didn't realize that Native American people still live in the United States and have a rich culture and history. When the local Seneca woman came to visit and show artifacts, many students were confused about how she could be alive. They thought she must be really really old since, in their minds, all Native people had died years ago. They didn't realize that there are nearly 600 Native American tribes in the United States currently and they each have their own traditions, history, and culture.

These challenges always crept up on me when it was time for my co-teacher and me to plan the Native American unit we were expected to teach every other year (our curriculum ran on a two-year cycle and we looped with our students). The year that this story takes place, I was teaching third grade with a different co-teacher and Teaching Assistant than I had taught the previous Native American units with. At the charter school, we planned and taught 3-month in-depth units called Expeditions. Since I was working with new partners and teaching a new grade level, we were starting from scratch with planning the unit.

It was the Teaching Assistant who mentioned Indigenous Peoples' Day. She had just heard a news story explaining that some places around the United States were making a change in what they celebrated the second Monday of each October. There was apparently a growing movement to honor the history of Indigenous People in the United States rather than the famous Italian explorer.

At the time of this story, we were into the second half of the 2010s. Upon further research, we all learned that Indigenous peoples first proposed the idea in 1977 at a United Nations conference. In 1989, South Dakota became the first state to switch Columbus Day to Native Americans' Day, and celebrated it for the first time in 1990. Since then, at least eight states and 130 cities across the United States have made the change.

We decided that we had a controversial topic on our hands that would be a perfect vehicle for teaching about Native Americans and for covering our ELA standards of reading and comprehending texts, writing opinion pieces, and participating in conversations with multiple exchanges. We planned to cover Native American content, including how they used natural resources, family roles, economics and government, and daily life. We also planned to teach about European contact. All the while, we would be encouraging students to think deeply about an engaging topic and communicate their opinion through writing and speaking.

We were excited to present our students with a controversial issue for them to take a stand on. So many times, adults don't realize that children are capable of thinking deeply about important issues. A lot of times, we water things down for children or present them with work that is just busywork, rather than authentic. The truth is, with careful planning and close monitoring, children can digest complex information and articulate their learning at a very sophisticated level.

Since the charter school was progressive, we had some leeway in our planning. We were able to design the unit so that we presented each side of the story: the history of Native People in the United States and the story of Christopher Columbus. We were careful to use reliable sources and present our third-graders with the information in a way that was informative and also developmentally appropriate.

After we had covered the Native American and Christopher Columbus content, we presented the controversy to the students. Like their teachers, they had never heard of Indigenous Peoples' Day. We researched the pros and cons for celebrating each holiday. At the same time, we introduced opinion writing and our discussion protocol, which was a version of a Socratic seminar.

We started by having students write brief opinion pieces on unrelated topics; favorite food, should cell phones be allowed in schools, etc. Likewise, we started having conversations about topics that required an opinion in order to practice the discussion protocol. These two activities allowed students to practice giving their viewpoint in writing and speaking on topics they were already familiar with and most likely already had an opinion on.

Once the content was covered and the foundations laid for the discussion protocol and opinion writing, we presented the students with their two big final tasks: writing an opinion piece on whether Columbus Day or Indigenous Peoples' Day should be celebrated and participating in a discussion protocol with adults on the night we showcased our learning to families. Can you believe we pulled the parents into this also? Well, we did! We were fortunate to have engaged parents. We sent home some readings about Columbus Day and Indigenous Peoples' Day; "homework" for the parents and a description of the discussion protocol. We pleaded for their participation.

And they obliged us! On the night of our learning showcase, parents, students, and teachers sat in a large circle. Each person was allotted three talking chips and had the readings in front of them to reference. When someone felt inclined to speak, they put a talking chip down on the table and could either give their opinion, disagree with someone who had already spoken, or piggyback on someone else's idea, making sure to reference a part of one of the readings to support their claim.

That night, I observed quiet students muster up the courage to speak. I watched outspoken students carefully think through their statements, as they were limited to only three. I marveled at the number of parents who had taken the time to read the articles and participate in the discussion. And I watched someone who is accustomed to presenting a case in front of a judge and jury have to use that same amount of effort to present his opinion to little eight-year-old Caleb, who, with his last talking chip, presented his rebuttal.

The joy in teaching overwhelmed me that day when I saw how passionate the students were about the history we had been learning about. Whenever I'm not sure if

I have the courage to speak up about something, I only have to think of Caleb with his bright eyes and dimples and perfect articulation, and I know that I can say what I need to. Likewise, whenever I doubt whether kids can handle something serious, I take a deep breath and know that as long as the scaffolding and adult supports are there, they definitely can.

You too can find joy in holiday debates.

1. Rethink how you teach common topics and units if you feel unsatisfied with how you've taught them in the past. There may be a different avenue or approach you can take in which you can cover the same content in a new, more engaging way. Be on the lookout for new ideas! They can pop up when you least expect it!

2. Be sure to present multiple perspectives when teaching history. History is the story of what happened in the past. A story is subjective, so whenever possible, use resources such as primary source documents, historians, and museums to make the story as factual as possible.

3. Teach kids to research and form opinions about important, authentic, contemporary issues. Foster confidence in your students so that they are comfortable articulating their opinions through their writing and speaking voices. Kids have a lot of important and insightful things to say. It's our job to lift up their voices for the world to hear!

Writing/Thinking Exercise

Think of a topic or unit you have taught in the past that you have been unsatisfied with. Research different ways to teach the topic by going on the Internet, reading a new book on the subject, or picking your colleagues' brains. Make a list of five new-to-you ideas for covering the topic and commit to trying one of them the next time that topic or unit rolls around. Who knows, you may witness the next great debate!

1. _____

2. _____

3. _____

4. _____

5. _____

6. _____

I commit to...

_____

_____

Strengthening Assignments:
Finding Joy in Student-Driven Projects and Activities

Throughout their school career, students complete thousands of assignments. A common formula for a lesson at any level is for the teacher to present information to the class in some way, shape or form and then for students to practice the skill or solidify their understanding through some sort of assignment. Essays, drill and practice worksheets, homework, group projects, long-term assignments, research projects, and the list goes on; students are always either starting, in the middle of, or turning in an assignment.

Assignments are definitely a necessary part of the school experience! Students need ways to practice and demonstrate their learning. An important part of your responsibility as a teacher is to teach the curriculum and cover the standards. The good news is that there are many roads that lead to the same destination: mastering the learning target.

Across the many levels I have taught, one similarity among all ages and abilities is that kids learn the most when they have a certain amount of academic choice in sub-topic, method for acquiring knowledge, or presentation of what they've learned. Of course, not every assignment is going to be a beautifully designed, student-driven project or activity.

For one thing, teachers, contrary to popular belief, do not have extra hours built into their day! No teacher is capable of crafting every assignment perfectly. Often, a previously used and tested worksheet will do the trick for helping students master the learning target. But, worksheet after worksheet after worksheet for years and years? That gets old and unengaging for everyone involved.

In this section of the book, you will find out how to introduce activities that are engaging, multi-level, connected to the curriculum, and have multiple purposes. You will read about young kids who, when supplied with "good stuff," find a way to use it that furthers their learning. You will read about how to harness student ideas and use them to fuel motivation, creativity, and curiosity. You'll even read about how an assignment to create a game helped a senior in high school understand the connection between the effort he put into something and his level of success.

The joy in teaching comes in many unusual assignments and projects in the following stories; a colorful, quirky board game, deceased insects on a windowsill, paper monkey costumes, and Ziplock bags stuffed with math supplies, to name a few. As you read this chapter, I'm sure that a few brilliant ideas will emerge for you like the butterflies in one of the stories that follow.

An Economics Board Game

While teaching Special Education at an urban high school, I had the opportunity to work with many interesting young people. As a consult and Resource room teacher, I had the benefit of working in small groups or one-on-one with the students. This allowed me to get to know them very well, and there were many students who I made connections with that year and helped to have a successful year. There was one student in particular who was quite a character, and his story culminates in a colorful, somewhat confusing, and of course, joyful economics board game.

Isaac was a senior who was in the Government class that I was a consult teacher in. He had a learning disability and some attention difficulties, but he was a capable kid. He had passed State exams and classes during his first three years of high school. When I met Isaac, he was wearing a shirt that he had gotten from a youth running group in the area. Being a runner myself, I knew about the group and started a conversation with him about running. That was the beginning of our connection.

At least a few times a week, we would exchange small talk about running. We'd talk about where we liked to run hills, what races we were doing, and running goals. Now, I like running, but Isaac REALLY liked it. I knew this not just because of our conversations, but because after each race he did, he would wear his race t-shirt, race bib, and participation medal to school. Remember this was a tough, large, urban high school and in the midst of it was a kid named Isaac proudly sporting the race gear he wore in his weekend community 5K. After the Reindeer Run, he even wore the antlers to school! Like I said, he was a character!

Isaac and I had developed a good connection through our running talks and that was what I used to help get him through his senior year. I mentioned that he had some attentional difficulties, right? Well, around November was the first time I got to see how his distractibility affected him. I started to notice that I would often see Isaac in the hall in the morning between classes. He'd pat me on the back, we'd talk running and then go on our way. The weird thing was that even though I'd see him early in the day and talk to him, come seventh period (Government class), he was nowhere to be found.

This went on for a few weeks and Isaac was falling further behind in the Government class, so I decided to figure out where he was going during the time he was supposed to be in my class. I went into the computerized system our school had and clicked on his name to look at his schedule and his attendance record. It turned out that he was skipping several classes a day. Actually, the only two classes he was going to regularly were his cooking class and a sports literature class. I printed his schedule and attendance record and tucked them into the bag I carried with me throughout the day. I couldn't wait for the next time I'd "run" into him in the halls!

The very next day, I had my opportunity. I was walking out of the copy room and there was Isaac. He immediately came up to me and started chit-chatting and then our conversation went something like this...

"Oh, Isaac, I'm so glad I ran into you. I wanted to talk to you about something."

"Oh yeah, what, are you running a race or something?"

"Actually I wanted to talk to you about your schedule and your attendance to classes."

"OH."

(Remember, we are standing in the hallway during passing time at a busy high school when I decided to have this conversation with him!)

"I printed out your schedule and your attendance record."

"You did what!?"

"Yeah, I have it right here."

"Oh boy."

"Yeah, so, it's weird, because I see you in the morning sometimes, but then you're not in class so I wanted to see what was going on."

"Oh, well, ahh..."

(Enter exhibits A and B, schedule and attendance record.)

You can imagine the rest of the conversation involved Isaac making excuses and uncomfortable grunts while I tried to depart some wisdom to him about how much the teachers and administrators care about him and his graduation from high school and how important it is to go to class.

Guess who was in Government class that day? Yep, Isaac. And he came pretty regularly for at least a few weeks after that hallway chat. His attendance to class went through phases during the year. Sometimes it was really good, and other times, not so much. Every so often throughout the year, I'd have to give him another pep talk about going to class, and then his attendance would get better again.

It was easy to give him these inspirational speeches because I saw him a lot! Soon, after our hallway encounter, he figured out what my schedule was and when I'd be in my resource room. He'd often come check in to tell me about his running or just to say "hi." I took full advantage of the fact that we had this connection.

Later in the year, I found out that he was failing his Algebra II class and it was a class he needed in order to graduate. While we were working together on his Economics binder in Government class, I thought I'd slip in another pep talk. That conversation went something like this,

"So how are your other classes?"

"Oh, um..."

"How is Algebra going?"

"Ah..."

"Are you going to Algebra class?"

"Well, no."

"You know you need that class to graduate, right?"

"Uh..."

"What's the problem with Algebra, besides that you don't go to class?"

What followed was a conversation with Isaac about how he found the work difficult so he skipped class to avoid it. He pulled piles of wrinkled, incomplete Algebra work out of his backpack. I looked at the work and told him I could help him during fifth period when we both had lunch. He smacked his hand on his forehead and said, "Oh man, all this time you could have been helping me?!"

After that, in addition to his check-ins, he would come see me during fifth period a couple times a week and we'd work on his Algebra. He was always grateful for the extra help and super polite. One time, he said he had something for me. He pulled out a package of free tissues he had gotten at the race he ran over the weekend! In all my years of teaching, that might be one of the best gifts I've ever gotten!

He seemed to be on track for graduation until about a month before the end of the school year when he went back to his phase of skipping classes and not turning in work. Time for another pep talk! He managed to work his way back to a passing grade in Algebra II by handing in a bunch of late work, so the last thing to accomplish before his graduation was the final project for Government class. He needed to make a board game centered around an economics theme.

All throughout the year, Isaac had managed to pass his classes by doing a minimum amount of work. By June, I had used up a lot of my patience and energy encouraging him to do what he needed to do to graduate. I had doubts about his ability to produce an economics board game that met the criteria on the rubric and would earn him a passing grade in the Government class, especially since most of the project was meant to be worked on independently at home. Thankfully, Isaac surprised me!

The day that the game was due, Isaac came in with a poster board decorated in 5 different colored squares with arrows pointing every which direction. One of the other students commented that it looked like a board for a popular online dance game! He also had a bag full of irregularly cut pieces of paper with questions and answers written in the same five colors represented on the poster board. He had asked Mr. Z., a science teacher, if he had anything he could use for game pieces and had procured 4 small birds in different colors. He even had a pair of dice and a scrap piece of paper with the title "Game Rules."

Most importantly, he had enthusiasm! He was more excited about his game than the day he wore the reindeer antlers to school. Everyone who had brought in their games set them up and gathered a few players to play the game. I asked Isaac,

"What are the five colors? I thought we only brainstormed four categories of questions."

"Yeah, there are only four. The black squares are jokes I made up. If you laugh, you have to go back to start."

"Oh, ok. So the categories are still Credit, Consumers, Supply and Demand, and Economic Systems?"

"Yep!"

He excitedly went through the rules with myself and the two other high school boys playing. He had the game board laid out and the cards all mixed up in a messy pile, sort of like when you play Go Fish. I determined that we should go oldest to youngest and took the first turn. My first question was about credit (the blue category). Isaac had to search through the disheveled pile for a blue card. There was one on top, so I said,

"Oh, there's one."

"No, they are numbered. I have to find Blue 1."

Throughout the game, I tried suggesting that he organize the cards into colors and the order in which they were numbered but he was too excited to hear my suggestion, so the game went on with him having to frantically search through the pile for each specific card. When we came to a black card, I thought I would have to think of something really sad so that I wouldn't laugh and have to go back to start. Then he read the joke. It made no sense. What. So. Ever. But, he was so proud of the jokes he had made up that the other two players and I just smiled and nodded.

After the "joke" and frantic searching for cards, I was ready for anything and I soon had my next opportunity to be confused/delighted. The orange category was Consumers. When he read the first orange question, "What breaks down dead organisms in an ecosystem?" I was confused. What did that have to do with economics? Then I realized that instead of searching for questions about Consumers in the economy, he had found an internet site with questions about Producers and Consumers in the Biology curriculum! I'm not sure if the other two students playing the game even noticed and Isaac was so excited that I couldn't bring myself to say anything about it.

As I was playing Isaac's confusing, colorful economics board game, I realized that this was the most effort I had ever seen him put into any assignment. His game may have been a bit odd with its disorganized cards and board, spattering of science questions, and bad jokes, but it was all his. For whatever reason, he had taken a great deal of pride in making that game and he ended up earning a passing grade on the assignment and in the class. At that moment, watching Isaac grin proudly as he shared his game, I knew that I was feeling the joy of teaching.

You too can find joy in an economics board game.

1. Don't be afraid to confront students about their misbehavior. As long as you have established a relationship with them and you speak with them respectfully, you are likely to achieve a positive outcome. Kids want to know that the adults have expectations for them.
2. Maintain expectations for your students even when you have to keep reminding them over and over again. Most of them eventually get the message.
3. Celebrate successes even when they aren't perfect. Hard work and effort deserve praise, especially when it's out of the ordinary for a student.

Writing/Thinking Exercise

Think of a student you have now or have had in the past who struggled to meet academic and behavioral expectations. List at least three successes they had.

1. _____

2. _____

3. _____

4. _____

5. _____

Dead Bugs

The look on the nature guide's face was priceless. I was co-teaching second grade at the charter school and we were studying local animals and habitats. We were visiting a local nature park and having a lesson on beehives. The guide had just shown us the inside of one of the empty hives and there were some dead bees on the bottom.

When I saw the dead bees, I thought about how amazing it would be to look at them under the high-powered magnifier we had just gotten that attached to the iPad. We could take detailed photographs and talk about the bee body parts. I imagined how some kids would be excited at seeing all of the little hairs on their legs, the translucency of their wings, and the bulge of their eyes. I also imagined how some kids would be thoroughly grossed out by those details. Both hypothetical reactions to the magnified dead bees seemed like incredibly valuable learning opportunities! So, without hesitation, I said,

"Could we have some of those?"

The guide looked at me with a confused expression and asked,

"Some of the dead bees?"

I held my ground and acted like this was a very common request.

"Yeah, they are so cool! We could look at them under the magnifier on the iPad and study their body structure! We could look at their bulging eyes and hairy bodies!"

At this point, some of the kids chimed in with comments such as,

"Oh, that would be so cool!"

Some of the kids just stared. They were used to their teachers being a little wacky. My co-teacher, an amazing woman, supported this crazy idea. She had ideas for how we could draw the dead bees and write stories about them.

The guide looked at me again and said something like,

"Well, no one has ever asked for dead bees before, but sure!"

Then she really got into it! She made sure to pick out the best specimens with the least damage to their bodies. She even found us a drone!

To understand how special a drone is, you need to know a little about the bee colony. You see, the bee colony is a caste system containing three classes of bees: the queen, the worker bees, and the drones. There is one and only one queen in the hive. She is a stereotypical queen in that her servants wait on her hand and foot. Her job is to lay eggs; lots of them. A queen can produce 1,500 eggs a day! She even controls the sex of the eggs she lays according to the size of the hive. As you can imagine, this royal bee with her long, slender body and working ovaries needs a lot of protection. That's where the worker bees come in.

Most of the bees in the colony are worker bees. They are the sterile females who do all of the work. They feed the young, make the honey and wax, clean the hive and protect it. They care for the queen by cleaning her, feeding her, and even removing her waste! Their bodies are smaller than the queen and the drone and contain a short abdomen, pollen baskets on their hind legs for collecting pollen, and a barbed stinger.

The last type of bee is the drone. They are the only males in the colony and their sole purpose is to mate with the queen. Once they mate, they die. If they fail to mate, they hang around for a bit to eat honey and pollen until the worker bees kick them out. The drone may lead a short, unfulfilling life, but let's not forget how special they are! They make up only a small percentage of the hive, so they are noteworthy simply because of how rare they are. They also have a different body than their female counterparts.

A drone is larger than the worker bees and about the same length, but heftier than the queen. He has huge eyes that cover the better portion of his head. And strangely enough, a drone has no stinger! But most importantly, although the queen gets most of the credit for keeping the hive going, without the drone and his seminal fluid and spermatozoa, propagation of the hive would not be possible.

The nature guide carefully handed us a few dead worker bees and a drone. I set them in an empty container from my lunch box as curious seven- and eight-year-old scientists looked on. When we got back to class, we set them up one by one under the magnifier on the iPad and projected it onto the screen in the classroom. SO COOL! My co-teacher and I had the kids do some detailed drawings of what they saw and then we moved on to the next part of our day. The dead bees were set safely on the windowsill for more examination another day.

The next few days went by as days in a second-grade classroom do. There was reading, writing, and math. There was socializing and social drama. But what made our classroom special was that there were also DEAD BUGS.

A little boy named Miles was the first to bring a dead bug from home. He brought in a handsome dragonfly with blue iridescent wings set inside a special container with a magnifying glass on top. The class examined his body, drew it, discussed it, and read about it. Did you know that adult dragonflies can capture their prey in the air due to their acute eyesight and high rate of speed while flying? The scientists in the room were hooked on dead bugs and the worlds that they opened up to us below and above ground.

The next specimen to come in was a cicada skin. Cicadas are very interesting insects indeed! The students learned that depending on the type of cicada, it either spends 4-7 years or 14-17 years living underground. Then it climbs a tree, emerges from its skin, and becomes an adult. The skin you find hooked to a tree is what is left over from the cicada's childhood.

Soon, the classroom windowsill was filled with dead bugs. In addition to the bees, dragonfly, and cicada, kids brought in dead ladybugs, moths, stink bugs, and even a dead fly. Gross. We had living bugs in the classroom too. We had an ant farm, which we had to keep adding more duct tape to the edges of because the ants were escape artists. We also had five painted lady caterpillars which eventually metamorphosed into butterflies.

As cool as the living insects were, the dead bugs were better. We could look at them up close using the magnifier and maneuver them to see different parts of their bodies.

Because they didn't move, we could spend a lot of time examining them. But mostly, the dead bugs were better because the kids were so into them.

Almost every day, someone else had found a dead bug in their window at home or along the sidewalk and brought it into the classroom to add to our windowsill insectarium. I often wondered if any of the parents thought it was odd that their kid brought a dead bug to school. Luckily, at that school, we had great, supportive parents who trusted that our methods would lead to their kids learning a lot and being happy at school, even if that involved dead bugs.

The end of the unit rolled around and it was time for the kids to plan how they would showcase what they learned during the previous three months about animals and habitats. They decided to set up the classroom like a museum, with different exhibits to present what they had learned. And you guessed it. One of the exhibits was the windowsill of dead bugs. The group in charge of that exhibit made labels for each specimen including the name of the bug and some information they deemed important.

We had 10 exhibits in all, so the dead bugs were just a small piece of the night, but I'll never forget that they were part of the showcase for families at the end of that year. Who knew I could find joy in something as weird and disgusting as dead bugs? When I first asked the nature guide for some of the dead bees, I didn't imagine the idea would take off. I figured we would look at the bee bodies, do some writing and drawing and that would be it.

The contagion of collecting dead bugs reminds me of a few things. First, if you are excited about something when you are teaching, most likely, the kids will get excited too.

Second, never underestimate the power of learning from something that seems commonplace. How many of us sweep or vacuum up dead bugs and never think twice about it? The second-grade windowsill insectarium reminds me that as a teacher (and a human being), I need to look for the extraordinary in the ordinary and get excited about it! When I do that, I can even find the joy of teaching in a lifeless housefly.

You too can find joy in dead bugs.

1. Foster a love of nature in your students. Studying the world around you is cheap and accessible, even if all you have is a field or a small flower bed in an urban neighborhood.
2. Have crazy ideas and ask unusual questions. You'll model curiosity, courage, and enthusiasm for your students and it will most likely catch on.
3. Celebrate the connections students make when they go home to what they are learning at school. Encourage them to bring these connections to school, whether it's a book or a dead dragonfly.

Writing/Thinking Exercise

Go outside and find a natural object that you wouldn't usually give a second thought to.

Draw the object below including as many details as possible.

Write a list of 3 adjectives to describe the object:

1. _____

2. _____

3. _____

Make a plan to help students notice natural objects in ways they usually wouldn't.

_____

_____

_____

_____

Paper Costumes

The years I spent teaching first grade (general education) were always extra exciting and terrifying because it was the year the kids learned to read. In Kindergarten, they learned their letters and sounds and to read emergent-level books with predictable text, but in first grade, most of them REALLY learned to read. That part was exciting. It was terrifying though, to start the year knowing that it was my co-teacher and my job to take these students from beginning readers to READERS!

One of the activities I loved to do with first-graders was reader's theater. I had lots of stories that I had found in reader's theater format for different levels. I found that it increased accountability for students, improved fluency, and bolstered enthusiasm for even the most reluctant readers. Basically, it made them better readers.

One year, I had a first-grade class that was really into reader's theater. They loved it like no other class I had ever had or have had since. Because they were so fond of reader's theater, I decided to have a local actress come in and teach them about character development and using your voice and body to portray a character.

The local actress, Jessica, was amazing. The first time she came, she chose a book about an old man who is very grumpy because he lost his shoes to help the students try acting out a character. I remember one little girl went over to the math materials and grabbed a yardstick which she pretended was a cane! And their grumpy old man voices were just amazing! If you've never heard a little six-year-old girl with a naturally high-pitched voice try to make her voice deep and gravelly, then you're definitely missing out.

Jessica came a few more times after that and had the students act out everything from *Frog and Toad* books to classics like *The Old Man and the Sea*. While Jessica was there, I watched a shy boy become an angry toad who lost a button and a girl who always followed the rules become a demanding old lady. Because of the acting lessons the students had with Jessica, our reader's theater became even more rich. The students were excited to act out lots of different parts and their reading was becoming more fluent and clearer by the day.

I don't remember how the paper costume phase started. I'm guessing that I had brought in some basic costumes for one of the reader's theater stories and the need for costumes exploded from there. During choice times, kids started making costumes for the reader's theater they were working on during ELA. At first, the costumes were simple. One kid taped a tail to his bottom to become a cat. Another student made some paper glasses and taped them to his face.

Soon, though, word of costumes got out and the frenzy began. More and more kids started making costumes and they were getting bigger and more elaborate. During choice times, there were paper, scissors, tape, and markers everywhere as kids made aprons and bonnets, assorted animal body parts, and royal robes. The TA had the wonderful idea to bring in some butcher paper in different colors so that kids could make larger costumes without having to tape 75 pieces of paper together.

Something magical happened next. Up until a point, kids were making costumes for the reader's theater they were working on during ELA. But then, one of the six-year-old leaders had a wonderful idea. She got a group of friends together, took a book that had different characters, and then she and her friends began working out who says what throughout the book. They literally made their own reader's theater out of a book they found in the classroom library!

Well, I bet you can guess what happened next. Yep, all of a sudden, during choice times, there were various groups of kids dressed to the nines in their paper costumes developing reader's theater out of classroom library books. One of my very favorite memories from this time came when I rang the bell to give a five-minute warning for choice time clean-up. I looked out at the class and was greeted by 10 first-graders wrapped in brown paper with tails and ears who were getting ready to act out *10 Little Monkeys Jumping on the Bed!*

The joy of that moment lasted for the remainder of the year. When it was our turn to plan and lead the school-wide weekly assembly, I bet you can guess what the class decided to present. Their plays of course! In front of the whole school, there were groups of children dressed in their paper costumes, reading their lines from the reader's theater they had developed together!

The only hiccup came when a little boy who was acting out *The Oxcart Man* with his group got nervous and ran off the stage. His fellow actors/readers were so surprised that half of them just stood there and the other half ran after him. Oh well, they were only six years old after all! Even when that happened, it didn't squelch the joy I felt as I looked at my class of six-year-olds dressed in paper costumes giving it their all on stage. Who knew that readers could emerge wearing paper butterfly wings?

You too can find joy in paper costumes.

1. Give students opportunities to engage in reader's theater or other dramatic endeavors in the classroom. You never know which shy kid is an actor or actress in disguise. Drama also gives students a different avenue to learn and express what they know.
2. Make sure your students have time and materials to explore their own projects. Establish a classroom culture that encourages students to work together on their creative endeavors.
3. Provide students with audiences to perform in front of. It boosts their confidence, builds courage, gives them a sense of purpose, and provides them with a satisfying product to culminate their hard work.

Writing/Thinking Exercise

No matter what level or subject you teach, there are stories in your curriculum. List three texts your students encounter during their time with you and describe ways they could act out or experience the text in different ways.

1. _____

_____

_____

2. _____

_____

_____

3. _____

_____

_____

Counting Objects and Shoving them in Bags

During one of the years that I co-taught Kindergarten at the charter school, we had many kids who liked to make suggestions. They had all kinds of ideas for songs to sing, books to read, celebrations to have, projects, activities, etc. My co-teacher and I could have stopped wasting our time planning and filled each day with the kids' recommendations and we would have had more than enough material to last from 8 am to 3 pm for at least a month!

As much as we loved their endless ideas, we realized we couldn't just ditch the schedule and curriculum in order to indulge them. We also could no longer spend the whole day fielding questions that began with "When can we…" or comments that started with, "I know a great idea…." We needed to find a way to give them the freedom to propose their ideas without interrupting the schedule of the day and the curriculum we were supposed to teach. So… we introduced The Idea Box!

Physically, The Idea Box was quite beautiful. It started as an ordinary five-dollar wooden box from the craft store. My artsy daughter, who was about 12 at the time, decorated the box with tissues she tie-dyed, blue and pink paint, and about three coats of modge-podge. On the day of the introduction of The Idea Box, we ceremoniously placed it in the middle of the circle at Morning Meeting. We made a big deal about how beautiful it was; colorful and shiny; and how special it was that my daughter had made it just for our class. I think we may have even done a dance around it!

We told the students that this stunning box was now one of the most important objects in our entire classroom because it was going to be used for them to put their ideas in. Applause and cheers erupted from the crowd of five- and six-year-olds before us with the enthusiasm rivaling the moment a celebrity walks out on stage. We knew this box was going to be the answer to this particular classroom dilemma.

At our initial presentation of The Idea Box, we explained to the students that there were specific times of the day when they were allowed to write down their ideas and put them inside the box. There were also certain times of the day when teachers would sit with the class and check the box and honor the ideas. We showed them the little pieces of paper next to the box to write their ideas on and the symbols on the daily schedule that meant either it was a good time to put something in the box or it was a time the class would check the box together.

And the system worked beautifully! Every time a tug on one of our arms came, followed with the words, "I know what we should do..." we directed them to The Idea Box. For the first few weeks, most of the ideas were standard. A new book to read, a silly song, a game someone wanted to play, etc. The kids were ecstatic that we were honoring their ideas and life in Kindergarten was good.

Then someone wrote on one of the little pieces of paper, "Guess how many cubes are in the bag?" I remember reading the idea and being confused so I read it again,

"Guess how many cubes are in the bag?" The class stared up at me from the carpet looking for an explanation. I had none. I turned the paper over, looking for clues as to who wrote this idea or what it meant. Nothing. I was just about to ask the class who had written the idea when finally, one of the mathematicians in the class, a little boy with eternally messy hair and speech that went faster than he or anyone else could keep up with, woke from his daydream, jumped up and said, "That's my idea!"

The writer of the idea then ran to his mailbox and came back with a gallon-sized Ziplock bag stuffed full of the linking cubes that we used for math manipulatives. He took a spot in front of the class and explained that he wanted people to guess how many cubes were in the bag. He started calling on people and writing their guesses on the whiteboard! All the while, my co-teacher, the TA, and I just watched, wondering if he was going to go into a full-fledged math lesson. Maybe we should offer him a copy of the standards or suggest an end assessment?

After he got all of the guesses on the board, we asked him, "So, how many are in the bag? This is exciting! Did anyone get it right?" He said he'd tell us later. It seemed the little mathematician, being stereotypically absent-minded, had forgotten how many cubes were in the bag and needed to recount! We took advantage of the moment and counted the cubes together, focusing on putting them in groups of ten. That was the start of finding the joy in counting objects and shoving them in bags.

We had to stock up on plastic Ziplock bags. Everyone was stuffing anything and everything into plastic bags! The shelves were practically empty because all of the blocks, cubes, crayons, toys, markers, etc were shoved into bags that were then stuffed into mailboxes. Papers were exploding out of the mailboxes and strewn about because the mailboxes were full of Ziplock bags full of stuff. A thousand tiny notes that said "Guess how many (fill in the blank) are in the bag?" were crumpled into The Idea Box.

One day, my co-teacher threw out a bunch of pistachio shells that she found in someone's mailbox. You guessed it. A few days later, out of The Idea Box comes, "Guess how many pistachio shells are in the bag?" The little boy didn't have a bag, so he had just set the shells in his mailbox. Oops.

For the grown-ups in the room, guessing how many _____ were in the bag got tiresome. We were sure that the kids would lose interest eventually, but we were wrong. That fun activity lasted until the end of the year. So, we went with it. We worked on estimation skills, place value, skip counting, size, counting to and past 100, etc. I do believe that class had the best number sense of any Kindergarten in the county that year. That's how we found the joy in counting objects and shoving them into bags!

You too can find joy in counting objects and shoving them in bags.

---

1. Welcome student ideas. When you feel flooded by ideas, create a structure for sharing that will work in your classroom and setting.
2. Give students a chance to take the lead. You never know what impromptu lessons they might come up with that could set a fire for learning more under the rest of the class.

3. When you, as the teacher, start to feel bored with something the students are interested in and want to end the activity or project, don't. Hang in there. Remember that for kids, especially young kids, so much is new and exciting and they learn from trying the same thing out in different ways over and over. To us grown-ups, it may be tiresome, but to them, it's the way they solidify what they know and understand about a particular topic.

Writing/Thinking Exercise

Start your own teaching idea box. Get or make an attractive box. As you go through the year, add ideas that you have that you want to try the following year. In August, when you start planning for the year, open your idea box and make a plan to implement some of your wonderfully amazing ideas!

Around the World

A crisp October day, a steamy cup of coffee, and a warm conversation with an old friend; that's how this story begins. Julie and I had been in each other's lives for a while. At one point, our oldest daughters had been best friends, although the friendship faded when they went to different schools in seventh grade. My youngest daughter and Julie's middle child had also been in the same class from Kindergarten through sixth grade, and I had been her youngest child's teacher in Kindergarten, first and third grades.

Somewhere along the way, we became the kind of friends who met up every so often for coffee and conversation. On this particular morning, I was telling her about my new class at the urban high school. The students all had intellectual disabilities, as well as a host of emotional troubles and trauma in their lives. I was enjoying the job, but there were definitely challenges.

I was prattling on, the way I sometimes do, telling her about a sad situation with a student in my class and an annoying situation with the school I was in. The class I was teaching was a life skills class, however, our grocery funds had been revoked for the moment and there was no way to purchase food for cooking lessons. All of a sudden, I looked across the table to see my dear friend crying.

"Oh my goodness, I didn't mean to make you cry! We are fine at school. Let's talk about something else!"

And so, we spent the rest of our coffee date telling silly stories about our own kids and then lamenting on the chores we had to accomplish that Saturday.

About a week later, I heard a knock on the door and there was Julie. She explained that she had felt so moved by what I told her that she wanted to do something for my class and had bought us a gift card to the local grocery store.

"Oh, that's so nice of you, but you didn't have to do that. I told you, we are good!"

"I want to," she said. "Those kids are lucky to have you."

"Well, thank you," I said. "I really appreciate it."

I took the card, we exchanged niceties and said goodbye. After I closed the door, I opened the envelope the card was in and nearly had a heart attack when I saw the amount. I ran back outside in my bare feet and knocked on my friend's car window.

"This is too much!" I insisted.

Julie told me that she really wanted to give it to me and she knew I would make good use of it. For the next week or so, I plotted different ways to give her the card back. Then one day, I had an idea.

One morning during check-in time, Carlos and Sam were in the back of the room, looking at the map and discussing the places they were from; Cuba and Puerto Rico. As I watched them point to the map and marvel at how close their homelands were to each other, the idea came. Usually my best ideas come to me in the shower or when I am running, but this one popped into my head at about 7:25 one ordinary day.

When the students left for their PE class that morning, I told my TA and paraprofessional that we needed to have a quick meeting. I told them about the gift card and the idea I had that morning. I explained that after watching Sam and Carlos at the map, I thought we should take them 'around the world' through cooking.

My idea was that each month or so, we would study a new place. The students could research the place, write about it, and create artwork related to it. Each week, they would cook a dish from that place during our cooking time. Throughout the year, we could compile the writing, artwork, and recipes and even have the students review the foods they ate. By the end of the year, we'd have a cookbook with recipes and information from all of the places we studied. My TA and paraprofessional were on board, and the three of us were bursting with excitement for our upcoming journey around the world.

We started the adventure the very next week. We explained to the students that we had received a very generous donation to the local grocery store from a friend of mine. We discussed the value of contributing to the community when you are able to. We also talked about the importance of showing gratitude when you get a gift. We explained the project we planned to implement using the money and helped the students write thank you notes to my friend.

We started our trip around the world with a stop in Cuba. The next month, we landed in Puerto Rico. It was important to start with these two places because it demonstrated that we valued the cultural diversity of the members of our class. Sam and Carlos were excited to share what they knew about their heritage and offered ideas for recipes we should try. For one of the Cuban dishes we cooked, we sent home a sample to Carlos's guardian and asked him to write a review for our book. He gave it five stars!

Because of the severity of their disabilities, the students in this class were not required to take the culminating exams required of most students in the state where I lived. As a teacher, however, I was responsible for teaching them according to a modified set of state standards. Whenever I design a cool project or assignment for kids, it's very important to me that the experience is not only fun and exciting, but also educationally enriching and aligned to the standards. This project was no different, and I spent a lot of time checking and rechecking the standards and making alignment charts to make sure that I was covering the ELA, Social Studies, and Independent Living Standards as we traveled around the world.

I'm glad that the project aligned to standards, but the bigger benefits were often outside of what I could measure with a goal. Throughout the experience, students and teachers not only learned about the cultural diversity in the class, but came to understand the commonalities and differences of places all over the world. We learned that almost every country we studied had a favorite sport, that food and holidays were often unifiers, and that music often plays a big part in defining a culture.

The best days were our cooking days, which were every Monday, eighth and ninth period. The day would begin with Tahj asking, "What we cooking today?" practically before the day even began. We cooked all kinds of ambitious dishes from around the world; full Irish breakfast, sambusa, empanadas, honey bread, and so on. The day we made hummus, one of the girls said, "I want mine without the beans." At first I was confused, then I realized that she meant the chickpeas! I explained that the chickpeas were pretty much the entire food! Out of eleven students, only one had tried hummus before that day! Everyone, even the "no bean" girl, tried at least a taste that day.

Finally, towards the end of May, we put a halt on studying new places. Throughout the year, we had compiled all of the recipes and reviews, research and writing, and artwork, but the document needed a lot of touching up. In small groups, we tackled parts of the book and cleaned it up. We then emailed Mr. T., the Media teacher, to ask him if he could print and bind our more than 100 page masterpiece. We were all so excited when we got his email back saying "Yes!" We would each be getting a copy and he agreed to make a few extras for the life skills department and library.

I remember the day that the books were delivered. We stopped what we were doing and marveled at what we had created. All of the student writing, artwork, recipes, and reviews were there. Leroy, a 15-year-old who thought he was an old man, stroked his imaginary goatee and remarked, "Hmm, this is some of our finest work!" Tina was excited because one of the countries we studied was Saudi Arabia, which had been her idea since she had close friends who had immigrated from there. She was eager to show the book to her friends.

As I silently giggled about "the old man's" celebration of our book and smiled at Tina's enthusiasm, I knew then that I had found the joy in teaching once more. The fact that a class of students with severe intellectual disabilities could feel so invested in a project and create a beautiful end product was amazing. What's more, it all started with coffee and conversation and an unexpected donation. This experience reminds me to never underestimate what students are capable of. It also reinforces for me the power of kindness. Whenever I am lucky enough to get a donation, I will always make sure to do the most good possible with it.

You too can find joy in traveling around the world with your students.

1. Many people have a high regard for teachers and what we do. Tell your friends and family about the work you do and your students. You never know when someone might offer you funds, free stuff, or other support for your class. If you are lucky enough to receive a gift from someone, accept it with gratitude and use it to do the most good possible with your class.

2. Provide students with opportunities to do more than they think they can. Give them the chance to create products they are proud of and invested in.

3. Teach students about the cultural diversity around them and beyond. Many people have a small view of the world. Expand it for your students! Show them that the world is big, but despite the differences among people, we are more similar than we realize.

Writing/Thinking Exercise

Imagine that you are given a generous donation. Think about your students and what they are curious about. Review your curriculum. How could you use a generous donation to enhance your curriculum and connect with your students' unique interests?

_____

_____

_____

_____

_____

_____

_____

_____

_____

_____

Enhancing Classroom Management:
Finding Joy in Creating a Positive Environment

Many teachers will tell you that classroom management is the most difficult part of being a teacher. Lots of teachers have great ideas for engaging activities that make the curriculum come alive. Most teachers care deeply about their students. But few teachers will say that they feel confident in their classroom management. Most of my teacher friends have had the same recurring dream where the class is out of control and you, the teacher, are shouting like a maniac and chaos ensues. Fear not, it is only a dream!

In addition to the out-of-control classroom, which is almost always worse in your dreams, there are many other classroom management issues that teachers face. The following is a non-exhaustive list:

- Students who won't clean up
- Bullying
- Unengaged or unmotivated students
- Students who are not where they are supposed to be when they are supposed to be there

- Students who are disruptive and derail the class
- Students who are disrespectful
- Students who are angry or highly emotional

Please don't feel intimidated by the amount of classroom management issues that seem to plague teaching. It's true that classroom management is difficult, but as you grow as a teacher, you get better. There are many strategies, simple ideas, and routines that can be implemented and will turn your chaotic nightmare into a positive classroom environment.

In this section, you will read stories about how there is even joy to be found in classroom management. You'll read about a simple idea that made a big difference. You'll learn about how important modeling, routines, and expectations are. You'll learn about how explicitly teaching about bullying can change a classroom culture. And hopefully, you will be inspired to problem-solve with students in new ways.

Paper Stop Signs

At the ripe age of 22, right out of college, I landed a job in a high-poverty neighborhood as a Universal Pre-K teacher. There was only one problem and it was a pretty big one; I had no idea what I was doing. Yes, I had a degree from a reputable college and provisional certifications in Elementary and Special Education. That didn't mean I had a clue about how to manage a class of 21 four-year-olds, communicate effectively with a group of parents who were culturally and economically different than me, and supervise two teaching assistants.

If you are reading this and you are a first-year, or even a fifth-year teacher, and you feel like you have no idea what you are doing, don't worry. That's normal. Someday, if you stick with it for 20 years, you will feel confident in your abilities as a teacher approximately 60% of the time. After over 20 years, I have some amazing days when I feel completely in-sync with the students and effective as an instructor. I also have days when I still feel like I have no idea what I'm doing. Luckily, those days get fewer and further between as each school year passes.

Let's get back to the story now. The Universal Pre-K class was part of a family resource center. I actually had a class of three-year-olds and a two-year-old class also, but this story is about the Universal Pre-K (UPK) four-year-old class.

At the time, UPK was new to the educational frontlines in the state where I live. The idea was to provide high-quality, free preschool education five days a week to low-income children and families to foster literacy and numeracy development as well as social skills in young children before they entered Kindergarten.

As a young, energetic teacher who had done one 10-hour practicum in a rural preschool, I envisioned myself singing with well-behaved children and engaging them in playdough creations, and then sitting in a teacher chair while they looked at me eagerly and listened quietly to the book I read to them. I imagined art projects where everyone created pieces that represented their true selves and circle times when we bonded as one big happy family.

Some of that did happen, eventually. Part of my initial struggles may have been because of the structure of the family resource center. My inexperience also contributed to my difficulties and the feeling of being overwhelmed. I was the only teacher in the building. There were some other programs housed in the building as a part of the family resource center, such as a program for young expecting mothers and a parent education program, but there were no other teachers there I could get guidance from.

There were three other family resource centers in different parts of the city and each of them had a preschool with one teacher also. We met once a month at a bagel shop to bounce ideas off of each other, problem-solve, and bond with each other. As much as I enjoyed the camaraderie of those "meetings," I definitely would have benefitted from something more structured like a mentor or at least a teacher next door to help me.

So, what did I need help with? Well, basically, I was pretty good at coming up with fun and educational ideas, such as following recipes to address math skills and using flashlights to make shadow puppets as a way to teach the science concept of light and dark. I understood what curriculum I needed to deliver in order to meet the goals of UPK. I even had a pretty good handle on activities that were developmentally appropriate for young kids. As a former camp counselor, I knew a plethora of silly, kid-friendly songs.

The problem was, the kids were all over the place! I had a circle time when they first came in, but I spent most of the time trying to get them out of the housekeeping and block areas. During project times, kids wandered around and did all sorts of wonderful things like hide under tables. The classroom was well-stocked with supplies and I had failed to set any guidelines about their use. Consequently, children were doing anything they wanted whenever they wanted to. The director had purchased a brand new, kid-sized tool bench and kids just randomly went over and banged a hammer on it throughout the day. It was chaos.

Still, I pressed on. In January of that year, I began taking my first early childhood education class in the evening for my master's degree at a local college. That was so helpful! I don't even remember what class I started with, but I remember making connections with other teachers who taught preschool. As I described my struggles with classroom management to a fellow classmate, she suggested a simple idea; paper stop signs. She said that in her class, when an area of the room is closed, she puts up a paper stop sign and the kids know not to use that part of the room.

She also explained how she explicitly introduced the paper stop signs to the students.

The next week, I made a whole bunch of paper stop signs out of construction paper. On Monday morning, when the students entered, the only part of the room that was open was the mini carpet area we used for circle time. The rest of the room was plastered with about 20 paper stop signs. I remember three little girls running to the housekeeping area, seeing the stop sign, and then stopping and hugging each other. I walked over and explained to them that the sign meant to stop and go to their carpet spots. Surprisingly, they did!

My new friend's simple suggestion about using paper stop signs had actually worked. Next, I employed her second piece of advice which was to explicitly introduce the signs. At our circle time, I talked about the signs and then showed students how if they were walking to an area and saw the sign, they had to stop and go to a place without a sign. I actually got up and modeled this. For the next week or so, I only opened one or two sections of the room at a time, and I kept the others closed off. Little by little, as the weeks went on, the class felt more in control and it was easier to implement projects and activities with the kids.

This experience was the first time I realized how important it is to have clear expectations for students, no matter the age or setting. Since then, I've gotten a lot better at setting expectations! Just last week, I had a fantastic beginning-of-the-year discussion with my new class of high school students, all of whom had intellectual disabilities, about the rules we should have for the classroom. It took a long time for me to learn how to effectively manage those kinds of conversations.

As a 22-year-old UPK teacher, I did not have the skills I have now in classroom management. Luckily, back then, I had a classmate who suggested that a red paper octagon and a discussion could help me achieve at least some semblance of order. When I think back on that year, I not only feel joy for the paper stop signs that calmed the storm, but also for the help I got from someone I barely knew. The lesson in this story is twofold; one, a simple idea and a clear explanation can help solve a problem in the classroom, and two, teachers need one another.

You too can find joy in paper stop signs.

1. Teaching is hard, especially when you are just starting out. Don't give up. Connect with your colleagues and ask for help. Even a veteran teacher knows that "we're all in this together."

2. Set clear expectations and routines for students and be consistent. Kids need to know what is expected of them in regards to how to treat each other, work expectations, and care of materials. Model what you would like them to do and how you want them to behave.

3. When faced with a classroom management issue, be willing to try new ideas, even if they seem simple. You won't know if it works unless you try it. Doing something to try to fix an issue is usually better than doing nothing at all.

Writing/Thinking Exercise

Write a list of at least three people who you can turn to for support when you feel overwhelmed as a teacher.

1. _____

2. _____

3. _____

4. _____

5. _____

6. _____

7. _____

8. _____

Lego Discussions

Early in my career, I spent three years as a middle school life skills teacher. In addition to dealing with the hormonal roller coaster called puberty that youngsters ride throughout middle school, my students also had emotional and intellectual disabilities. Additionally, many of them had chaotic home lives or traumatic histories.

As you can imagine, there was often distasteful language being tossed around the room. Objects were occasionally thrown. Learning to solve problems calmly and productively was a life skill we worked on daily, both preventatively through explicit lessons and as follow-up discussions to the many incidences we had of disruptive behavior.

Now that you have an image of 12- and 13-year-olds with emotional issues, swearing up a storm or punching a door, picture something different: a group of students sitting together on the floor creating elaborate Lego cities complete with roads, houses, hospitals, stores, and castles. Surprise! It is the same group of people, just at very different moments.

Despite all of the issues my students had, one thing they all loved was creating with Legos. During the half hour that we had of free time each day, many of them would choose to build together. Arguments during this time were infrequent and it was a positive and productive time of the day; something they could manage independently. That is, until it came time to clean up.

I allowed them to keep the large buildings and objects they created intact each day so that they could be worked on the next day, but I required that loose Legos be picked up and put in the bin. Sounds simple, right? For some reason, these kids could not get it together enough to pick up the Legos.

They would be working nicely together and then when time was up, they'd all disappear from the Lego area and refuse to clean up, leaving the floor strewn with annoying tiny bricks. Legos were everywhere, and those things hurt when you step on them! Not to mention that it is quite embarrassing when the principal comes in to observe and there are Legos on the floor. Something had to be done.

At the same time, I was going to graduate school part-time in the evenings to earn my master's degree. Nowadays, many teachers in my state go to graduate school right after they get their bachelor's degree, but in my day, it was common to start teaching as soon as you finished your undergraduate degree and obtain a master's degree by going to school in the evenings. Although it was challenging to be in school and teach school at the same time, the advantage was that I could try out a lot of what I was learning in my graduate classes with my students.

In one of my classes, I was learning about "creating the democratic classroom." A democratic classroom is one in which the teacher holds class meetings and engages the students in problem-solving, encouraging them as valued citizens to take responsibility for making the classroom a good place to learn and be social. The democratic classroom seemed like the answer to our Lego woes.

So, one day, I sat the class down around the table and explained that we were going to have a class problem-solving meeting because we had a problem. I set the norms for the meeting: Speak one at a time, speak and listen respectfully, offer ideas. Then I introduced the problem: cleaning up those darned Legos.

I asked for solutions and wrote the ideas on chart paper. This may all seem very simple, but remember, this was a class of 8 students who had significant emotional and intellectual needs. They were not accustomed to having discussions in which they were the ones to offer ideas. Their first few ideas were pretty straightforward,

"We should clean up the Legos."

"We can pick the Legos up when we are done."

As I listened to their "ideas," I wasn't sure if the democratic classroom was going to work in this case. The conversation seemed to be going nowhere. Still, I prodded and prompted, and eventually, students came up with a plan. I would give them a warning 5 minutes before clean-up time, then everyone who had played with Legos at all during that time, even if they had left to do something else, would help clean up. That seemed like a good plan, but of course, it only worked some of the time, so, we held more meetings.

We discussed what was going well and what problems were still occurring. We came up with a list of solutions and from there, made a plan. Eventually, after five or six class meetings, we had a plan that included the clean-up warning, clear expectations for who had to clean up and what to clean up, and consequences for not cleaning up. The Lego problem was basically solved. The students continued to create their amazing Lego creations AND the floor was no longer an embarrassment.

The year following the Lego discussions, I was interviewing for the job at the charter school. The interview team asked me to describe a time when I had experienced a classroom management issue and what I did about it. I immediately thought of how I had created a democratic classroom in response to the Lego mess. As I described my students, the problem-solving meetings, and the number of tries it took to solve the issue, I remember many of the people on the interview team, who would later be my colleagues, nodding and smiling.

They laughed a little too, because let's face it, holding a series of meetings to solve a problem like cleaning up Legos is kind of absurd. To be honest, throughout the process, there were many times that I wanted to do one of three things:

1. Shout, "Just pick up the Legos, it's not that hard!"
2. Throw all of the Legos away
3. Pull my hair out and bang my head against the wall at the same time.

Thankfully, I didn't do any of those things! I kept at it, because deep in my heart, I knew that if the students felt like their voices and ideas were heard, they would eventually take ownership in the classroom. And they did.

Knowing that those students, who had severe emotional and intellectual disabilities, felt like valued members of a community that year brings me joy. It reminds me that no matter what age or type of class you have, engaging in productive problem-solving meetings is always possible, because every person needs to feel heard and valued.

You too can find joy in Lego (or other classroom) discussions.

1. Treat every student with respect and kindness. No matter what. Take into account their disabilities, home struggles, and any other circumstances and provide them with the care and effort you would want for your own children, nieces, nephews, grandkids, etc.
2. Have classroom problem-solving discussions with your students, no matter what age or level they are. Create or use an existing protocol, teach it to the students, and hold meetings when something arises that needs discussion.
3. Capitalize on your behavior and management issues. School isn't just about academics; it's about learning to live a good life and be a productive citizen. Use the behavior and management issues you have in your class to authentically teach students and help them practice characteristics of good citizenship.

Writing/Thinking Exercise

Think of a problem you have with your current class or with a class you have had.

Name the problem...

_____

_____

_____

Now imagine you are conducting a class problem-solving meeting. What are three solutions you think the students may come up with?

1. _____

_____

2. _____

_____

3. _____

_____

Birthday Cupcakes

One seemingly ordinary October day when I was teaching third grade, I noticed a little girl drop a piece of paper on the floor, turn her face to a sour expression, and loudly state, "Eww, Faith touched it!" The six or so other third-graders near her all made similar icky faces and uttered comments like hers. All of a sudden, I was reminded of kid movies I've seen and tween books I've read, where one misfit child is thought to have some 'cootie disease' and none of the other kids will touch them or anything they come in contact with.

Whenever I saw those movies or read those books, I truly believed that those things didn't actually happen in real life. Real kids are not that mean. But that sad day in third grade, I was proved wrong. Right under mine and my co-teacher's noses, a bullying situation I thought was only fictional was occurring in our classroom.

As soon as I realized what was happening, I told my co-teacher and we immediately called a class meeting. And I mean, *immediately*. I believe we were in the middle of English Language Arts when we had everyone clean up, without even a warning bell, and come to the meeting spot. We asked our teaching assistant to take Faith out of the classroom to do a job for a while and sat down with the class with our most serious and disappointed faces on to begin healing our classroom culture.

I described to the class what I had witnessed. We had 34 kids that year. We had sent Faith out of the room, which meant we had 33 sets of eyes on us. Of those 66 eyes, some of them looked right at us in sadness, some in disbelief and confusion, and some lowered with guilt. Heads both nodded and shook. No eight- or nine-year-old interrupted the teacher or said anything until we asked for comments and suggestions on how to fix the problem. Then the flood gates opened.

During that meeting, some kids described how this issue had been going on since the previous year. They explained that if Faith sat in a chair, some kids would let the others know she sat there, indicating that no one else should sit there. When she touched something, they warned others not to touch it. One boy said that it "always made (him) feel uncomfortable, but he didn't know what to do about it." Some of the students voiced that they didn't know this had been happening, but they felt bad about it. It was easy to see who was involved firsthand in the issue because they sat quietly.

Faith was a sweet girl who struggled academically and had trouble with cleanliness. Until I witnessed the paper incident and we sat down as a class for this meeting, I had noticed that she didn't have many friends, but to me it seemed that most kids just sort of left her alone. As I sat in that meeting and listened to kids describe things they had seen other kids do, while other kids voiced their surprise and others sat guiltily, I felt at once sad, overwhelmed, and empowered.

I was sad that this was part of our class. As a teacher, I've always emphasized community building as part of my classroom management. At the beginning of each year, I spend about 6 weeks developing rules, routines, and expectations with students. I spend time getting to know them and having them get to know each other. We engage in interactive games, shared experiences, and reflection.

To find out that despite all of this work my co-teacher and I had done, about a third of the class was bullying a child who was different made me extremely sad. I also felt overwhelmed. If this problem had been going on for at least a year, it was going to take a lot of deliberate work with the class on accepting differences and recognizing and combating bullying in order to rebuild a positive community. But of course, my co-teacher and I knew that we must do that and we felt empowered by the students who voiced how terrible they thought the situation was and how bad they felt about it.

Over the next couple of months, we completed an anti-bullying curriculum with the class specifically related to relational aggression. We engaged in activities such as role-plays, games, discussions, and stories that taught the students how to recognize bullying and what to do if they witnessed it. We also focused on teaching the students about differences among people such as different types of disabilities, family, and cultural differences. We were able to incorporate some of this into our English Language Arts curriculum, but some of the lessons, we taught separately.

Even though it took time away from our never-ending pressure to meet state standards, we did it anyway. I'd rather grow a group of students who care about each other and treat others with respect than students who meet every single standard at an expert level but are not good citizens of the world. It seemed like the work we did was helping.

During the lessons, the students were receptive and said all of the right things, but it was hard to know if they were continuing to be kind during the times we weren't looking as closely, like recess and free time. From what we saw, Faith seemed to have a few girls who had befriended her and we never again saw an incident like the paper one. We hoped for the best and kept at it.

The year chugged along and soon it was time for parent-teacher conferences in early December. Among the parents who came in for a conference was Katie's mom. Katie was a well-behaved student who did what she was supposed to during class, liked to read and write, didn't have a ton of confidence in Math, and had a nice group of friends.

During the conference, Katie's mom mentioned that when the incident with Faith had first occurred, Katie had come home and told her mom all about it. She had been very upset that her classmates had been so mean to Faith and told her mom that day that when her birthday came at the end of January, she was going to ask Faith to help her pass out her birthday cupcakes. Kids only got to pick one person to help and Katie had a lot of friends. She could have picked any of several girls in the class, but she planned to choose Faith because, as she told her mom, Faith had never gotten to do it and everyone should get to be the cupcake passer sometime.

I nearly cried when Katie's mom told that story. I realized then that if Katie had been so affected by the incident, then it was likely at least some of the other students had as well. In watching our class and their interactions with Faith, it also seemed that at least some of the activities and lessons we did surrounding bullying and accepting differences had made an impact. We had taken something that started out as a serious problem and used it to launch a curriculum geared towards improving students' social and emotional well-being.

On the day of Katie's birthday, she brought her pink sparkly cupcakes in and we sang our school birthday song to her. She called for Faith to come up and help her pass out her precious birthday treat. There was a slight glitch in the plan when my co-teacher and I realized that Faith was with her OT teacher! I sprinted down the hall and told Faith she needed to come quickly to help Katie pass out her birthday cupcakes. I didn't even give the OT teacher a chance to object; I just whisked Faith away back to the classroom.

Katie's kindness gives me hope that it's possible to heal a classroom culture and reminds me that bullying should never be tolerated in the classroom. As I watched Katie and Faith smile, laugh, and pass out cupcakes on that seemingly ordinary day in January, I felt the joy in knowing that teaching about kindness and accepting differences in others was the most important thing my co-teacher and I had taught that year.

You too can find joy in birthday cupcakes.

1. Don't allow bullying. Ever. It's not just "kids being kids." It's aggressive, targeted, and meant to assert power over someone who appears weaker than the others. It's not okay for kids to bully, be bullied, or stand by and watch, and it's our job as adults to teach kids better ways of being. If you see bullying, discuss it with your students and staff and come up with a plan to tackle it.

2. Take time for your social curriculum no matter what age or level you teach, even if you only have limited time to do so. Teaching kids to be kind and good citizens benefits them and everyone around them in the present and the future.

3. Make sure that everyone has a friend. As Katie said, "everyone should get to be the cupcake passer sometime."

Writing/Thinking Exercise

Do a little research and find at least three resources you could use to teach kids about kindness and accepting others' differences. It could be a program, movie, book, quote, poem, meme, image, etc. List the resources and a brief statement of how you would use it in class.

1. _____

_____

_____

2. _____

_____

_____

3. _____

_____

_____

Blue Painted Plates, Recorded Rap Songs, and Spin Art Incentives

Most recently and currently, I teach self-contained Special Education at the high school level. After my first day in this position, I knew that not only would the class need the focused attention I've learned to give to setting up the class rules, routines and expectations, and community building during the first six weeks, the students would also need an incentive program to keep them motivated.

I'm not completely sold on reward systems, sticker charts, and token economies. Whenever possible, I believe it is better to foster intrinsic motivation in students through meaningful work, authentic audiences, and stressing the importance and benefits of being a lifelong learner. That being said, I don't judge anyone who uses a reward system with kids and I do believe that rewards can improve behavior and the quality of work in some students.

As I said, after my first day in this position, I knew I would need to develop an incentive program for the class. How did I know that? Well, in the first 6 ¾ hours that I knew them, there had been multiple accusations of other students "f..ing looking at me" from one girl, one boy had left the lunchroom without permission and wandered the halls, and I had been warned that one of the girls had had full-on tantrums all throughout the previous year.

On the second day of school, we had our first rules discussion, which actually was amazing. After they looked at me like I had two heads when I asked them to gather in a circle for a discussion, every student ended up participating and gave excellent ideas for important classroom rules. We continued with rules and expectations for about a week so that by the end of that time, we had an attractive poster with class expectations (Be Kind to Yourself and Others, Do Your Best and Learn A Lot, Be Respectful of Materials and Be Safe) including examples and images that every person in the class signed.

The poster gave us a concrete reference for what the expectations of the classroom were. We then went on to create other anchor posters, including ones for:

- How we wanted to treat each other and be treated throughout the year
- What the consequences would be for various offenses
- What we wanted to be able to do and learn at school throughout the year

My paraprofessional, Ms. Maloy, who had worked with Jasmine, the girl who threw tantrums the previous year, and who knew some of the other students, kept telling me that she couldn't believe how well the class was doing and how much she loved the way I built the expectations and community with the class. To me, I was just doing what I thought the class needed and what I have learned to do over the years. I've come a long way since the paper stop sign year!

So, on to the incentive program. I decided to create a Friday Fun jar. I had my best artist, Nick, draw a jar on yet another poster board and I copied some paper nickels, dimes, and quarters. I had the students in class with me for 5 periods a day, so I explained to them that if the class followed the expectations for the period with no more than one reminder, I would put a nickel in the jar. If by Friday afternoon, the jar had a total of 1.00, we would have Friday Fun. I showed them how we could trade in nickels for dimes and quarters throughout the week as well, so that we'd also practice money skills.

Next, I took a survey of what the students would like to do for Friday Fun. The idea was that for the last two periods of the day on Fridays, we would have fun together after a long week of working hard. I made a list of options including art projects, games, movies, cooking, outdoor time, science projects, and computer time. I told them to make a check next to any of the ones they would be interested in. Everyone checked off...you guessed it... movies and computer time, with a smattering of checks for the other options. Well, okay, I thought, we can start with a movie and popcorn, but I'll slowly introduce the other options once they get used to my quirky ways!

And that's what I did! As the year progressed, the students got used to all of my hands-on activities – quilt-making to teach about American history, various baking soda and vinegar projects to teach about chemical reactions and states of matter, the game of Life to practice turn-taking, money exchange, and reading skills, and so on – and they started to be more excited about trying out their own projects on Friday afternoons.

Some projects and activities were duds. One Friday afternoon, I showed the students various animals they could create by painting and cutting paper plates and adding objects such as googly eyes or pipe cleaners. I think a few kids made a fish, but the project wasn't a super big hit. Except for the blue paint! That day, Ms. Maloy and I discovered that Jasmine really liked to paint paper plates with blue paint. In fact, she used up almost all of the blue paint and a stack of plates at least half an inch thick that day.

As it would happen, by that point in the year, Jasmine had a personal behavior chart with built-in rewards. She benefitted from frequent check-ins and reminders for appropriate social behavior, so she never went back to having temper tantrums every day as she had the previous year. So, Ms. Maloy and I added painting as an incentive. Over the years, I've learned not to question things that work, even if they seem strange. As long as no one is getting hurt and learning is happening, then using a weird idea that works is ok by me!

I went out and bought more blue paint and paper plates and Jasmine often chose to use those materials when she earned free time. Ms. Maloy and I laughed privately at the fact that painting plates blue was like a magic fix for Jasmine. I often wondered what her mom thought of all of her blue-painted plates and what she did with them once she brought them home! I imagine one corner of her room must be completely filled with her blue masterpieces! Nonetheless, it was an incentive that worked for Jasmine and it reminded me that everyone is motivated by different things.

Another Friday, I brought in the old spin art maker and showed the students how to use it. I figured that a few kids might use it and enjoy it, then I'd bring it back home to store in my basement. Well, that spin art maker remained at school for the rest of the year because of Tina. Tina was one of my higher-level kids, reading at a third-grade level or so. She was generally well-behaved, but had a lot of emotional issues and missed a significant amount of school, usually one day a week.

The first day she tried the spin art maker, she made some average-looking art squares. Then, week after week, she started to experiment using different colors and amounts of paint and ways of dropping the paint. She even started using objects like toothpicks or popsicle sticks to make designs in the paint. Eventually she had such a large pile of spin art creations and was so proud of them that I bought her a small photo album to keep them in.

The last amazing incentive I'll tell you about is Tahj and his rap songs. Tahj looked up to rappers and tried to dress and act like one. Some rappers, like Tupac, are good influences for young people. Some, however, fall into gangs and are not good role models. Throughout the year, Ms. Maloy, Ms. Johnson (the TA), and I constantly battled with Tahj about appropriate school behavior while trying to honor his appreciation of rap music and steer him toward good influences. We even made a social story for him outlining appropriate school behavior.

Another student in the class, Leroy, also liked music, but an entirely different type: jazz and blues. He was sort of an old soul who often came to school dressed in suspenders and a fedora hat and played his harmonica during free time. During a class lesson about something in history, he would often say something like, "Well, back in my day..."

Sometimes it was hard to tell if it was an act or if he really thought he was 65 years old!

In any case, Leroy had learned how to record songs he created using a free online site and often chose to do so on Fun Fridays. When Tahj caught wind of this, he asked Leroy to be his manager and help him record rap songs! Tahj started writing raps in a notebook and practicing them while Leroy tried to avoid his incessant asking for help. Until one day he gave in. With the caveat that I write up a contract for them!

In the contract, Leroy specified that he would only help Tahj if he followed directions and acted appropriately for school. I used 'legalese' contract language and had them both sign it. It was all very official and started a several-week period of Leroy helping Tahj record rap songs during Fun Friday.

So, by the end of the year, there were times when the class who had wanted to "f..ing fight" or who had wandered away was unrecognizable, especially on Fun Fridays. Ms. Maloy, Ms. Johnson, and I would look around and see Leroy and Tahj recording music, Jasmine painting plates, and Tina making spin art, as well as other kids playing cards, talking, or laughing over something on the computer.

We had lots of hard days throughout the year; one girl stapled her finger, one girl threw her shoes at a security guard, and so on, but on Fun Fridays, I could look around and know that the joy in teaching was right in front of me in the smiles of the students who had earned the freedom to paint and rap their own way on Friday afternoons.

You too can find joy in blue painted plates, recorded rap songs, and spin art incentives.

1. Give each class a fresh start. No matter what you have heard about them from previous years, start the year with a clean slate. Establish rules, expectations, and a community with them and believe that your efforts will pay off, despite what you may have heard about the students' past behaviors.

2. Broaden your students' horizons. If you have a reward system such as Fun Friday with your class, little by little introduce them to projects and activities they may never have done if it weren't for you. Don't believe that kids just want to engage with screens when they have free time. You never know what they might create and do if you give them other options for how to spend their time and express themselves.

3. Once your students have developed some cool interests, support them! If fine arts is their thing, supply materials and help them find ways to display their work. If music is their interest, find ways they can record or perform their music. Do what you can to help them feel like real artists, musicians, athletes, gamers, scientists, etc.

Writing/Thinking Exercise

Think of a child you have or have had in class who would benefit from a reward system. List at least 5 activities they might be motivated to work towards.

1. _____

2. _____

3. _____

4. _____

5. _____

6. _____

7. _____

8. _____

Start to make a plan with the child for how they can earn one of the rewards. Identify the target behavior and write a brief statement describing how the child will earn the reward.

_____

_____

_____

_____

_____

_____

_____

_____

_____

_____

_____

_____

Cracked Eggs and Quarantine

I thought I had finished writing the content of this book about 6 months ago, however, I find that I must add just one more story (for now!). The joy of teaching often comes during unexpected and difficult situations. At this moment, people around the world are enduring a global pandemic. It is unexpected and difficult, to say the least. It is terrifying, deadly, and tragic. It should be more than we, as humans, can handle. However, every day there are stories of people rising up.

For educators, the experience has been many things; heartbreaking, frustrating, and unfamiliar. We left our classrooms one day and didn't realize it was our last with those students. We wonder if our students are okay; if they are getting enough to eat and how they are coping with the stress of this situation. We spend hours uploading lessons and learning new technology, only to be dismayed by poor attendance from students for video conferences and assignment completion. We are in unfamiliar territory. No one prepared us for this in college or professional development.

I feel the pain of this experience. Sitting in front of my computer is not where I want to be. I want to be physically *with* my students doing fun science experiments, engaging in deep discussions, and celebrating Spring together.

Despite the sad reality of this unprecedented time, I have been blessed with joyful teaching experiences during the past 8 weeks of quarantine. My guess is that if you are an educator reading this, you have also had moments of joy with your students during this difficult time. Please tell your stories; we need to hear them! Here is mine. First, though, let me give you a little background on pre-pandemic life in our classroom.

Picture this, sometime in October...

The bell rings. Some students have already arrived in the classroom. A few are gathered outside of the room and come in when I prompt them. 5 minutes pass. 6 out of the 12 students are still MIA. I locate 4 of them down the hall visiting with a favorite teacher. I discover that one is absent.

I call security to ask them to look for the other student who I assume is off making out with his girlfriend of the week. They find him and he claims he was at the nurse. A few minutes later, the nurse calls to ask for him since he has not come to get his medication yet. He has been in the school building for almost an hour.

Picture this, sometime in November...

I'm standing in front of the class getting ready to launch a science experiment. I have the materials and what I think is an engaging inquiry question on the board. I ask students to come up and help pour the liquids into beakers. Two of the students decide it is a good time to loudly call each other insulting names across the room. Another student throws a handheld pencil sharpener which crashes to the ground releasing shavings and graphite. One student, who likely just feels sorry for me, volunteers to help with the project.

Picture this, sometime in November...

We are in the Life Skills room cooking the meal that the students voted on: a full breakfast with eggs, banana muffins, and cut-up fruit. I have assigned a group of 4 students to make the muffins from a mix. They are all in the cooking CTE class and have loads of cooking experience. They are also all friends.

Suddenly, one of them gets angry about something that no one is aware of, throws a raw egg on the floor, and starts shouting, telling me I have mental problems. The stove is on and the cabinet containing the knives is open. The egg thrower storms out and, luckily, Security comes to find out what the fuss is all about. I wish I knew.

This year, for the second time, I am teaching a high school 12:1:1 class in an urban high school. My students have intellectual disabilities. Some of them have challenging situations in their personal lives or emotional difficulties. They are also teenagers complete with out-of-whack hormones trying to navigate a world that makes no sense. I've taught for 22 years in a variety of situations. You'd think I would have teaching figured out by now.

In my experience, usually it takes about 6 weeks for a class to settle in. This year at the 6-week mark, I had chaos. You might ask, "Why didn't you set up expectations?" I did. You might wonder, "Why didn't you do lessons on respect?" I did. You might think, "It sounds like there were no rules or consequences." Actually, there were. I did everything that I always do at the beginning of the year with this class, but it took me until mid-November to realize that this particular class needed something different.

My students had two main issues: they weren't buying into the importance and relevance of the learning and they hadn't connected with me or each other in a way that fostered a positive classroom community. In about mid-November, I realized that I needed to step back and reevaluate the situation. The kids were a mess and so was I.

I decided to change three aspects of the class in order to achieve better management and a more positive class community.

- I decreased the number of whole-class lessons I was doing.
- I set up an incentive program that would target problem behaviors.
- I started making a more conscious effort each day to recognize and acknowledge the positive things happening within the class.

In order to decrease the number of whole-class lessons I was doing, I taught the students how to use technology more fluidly. I started by making an individualized form that mirrored the morning calendar routine we had been doing as a class each day. I uploaded the form to Google Classroom and taught the students how to log in, complete the assignment, and turn it in. I had one student who was particularly tech-savvy and I employed her as the Technology Assistant. It took a few months, but eventually everyone was able to access and complete work independently in Google Classroom.

Decreasing the amount of whole-class lesson time is a practice I often forget about. Once all of my students were accountable to the morning calendar, they couldn't just talk and fool around while one person at a time went to the smartboard to complete a section of the routine. There was a lot less disruptive behavior and more learning. As a bonus, they became more efficient with technology, which would prove vital during the Covid-19 school closure.

With the help of my mentor, I set up an incentive program that focused on punctuality, politeness, and productivity. I called the program: P's for Pizza. During each period, individual students could earn a total of 3 "P's"; one for being punctual, one for being polite, and one for being productive. I made a huge chart that filled an entire wall to keep track of the "P's." I explained to the class that once they earned 6000 P's, which could take as little as two months, we would have a pizza party like no other.

To my delight, more than half of the class bought into the incentive right away. I could see kids running down the hall to get into the classroom on time and yelling "I'm here, Miss! I'm not late!" It was also easier to track who the main offenders of the troublesome behaviors were. The other students started to notice also and called them out on their behavior. They wanted that pizza! Four months later, we enjoyed pizza, soda, wings, and camaraderie. In addition to the group reward, I gave out individual acknowledgments to the students who had earned the most P's or improved the most.

Highlighting the positive was the third action step I took to mend the classroom management fractures we had. I made a bulletin board that said, 'Great Things Are

Happening Here!" I put up pictures of the class working on projects, cooking, and on the field trip we had taken to the local public market. With the evidence in front of them on the new bulletin board, the students could see that what we were doing in school wasn't all awful.

In addition to the new bulletin board, I made a conscious effort to call out positive academic and social happenings throughout the day, no matter how small. As an even bigger celebration of positivity and growth, I held a certificate ceremony in which students were recognized for what made them awesome. With the emphasis on positivity, slowly, the students started to feel like I was on their team and not just out to get them for being late or disruptive.

Picture this, sometime in January...

I'm sitting at my desk while students are in the room (a rare occurrence), looking through completed work. Joel, the former egg-thrower, approaches my desk.

"Miss, I'm so sorry."

"For what?" I ask.

"For all of the things I did at the beginning of the year. I just wasn't ready to be back in school."

I look at him and take half a second to ponder how to most effectively respond. "Joel," I say. "Life is kind of like a roller coaster. Sometimes you're at the bottom of the hill. I think you were there for a long time, struggling with school. I think you're going up now though, and that's awesome! I'm really proud of you and how far you've come. Keep going up."

"Thank you, Miss."

Picture this, mid-March, the day before Quarantine...

Our morning starts with a playfully competitive game of Black History Jeopardy. Students are in groups of three frantically looking up information on their Chromebooks to answer the questions before other teams. They don't need to look up every question, they know a lot of the answers already from all of our lessons and activities during Black History Month.

In the afternoon, we finish watching the movie "Selma" and have a sophisticated discussion about the Civil Rights Movement. Jason, who, in November, used science class to call his friend names, eloquently describes the injustices that Black people have endured over time.

On our morning news, we had been watching the coronavirus tear through Asia and Europe, plague cruise ships, and travel East across the United States to our part of the country. We knew that the virus had landed in our area, but none of us realized that this day would be our last together. Forever.

Just like that, the sanctuary of our classroom that was so difficult to create this year was gone. We, like the rest of the world, were forced to communicate through the space and wires between our houses. Distance learning has so many challenges. There are students without adequate technology, parents who are essential workers, and emotional responses to the situation that all make learning hard. So hard. But through the Covid-19 closure, with this group of students who were so challenging for so long, I have found that there is even joy in teaching during Quarantine.

The former egg-thrower...

During the first three weeks of distance learning, Joel, the former egg-thrower, is my biggest surprise. He completes every single Google Classroom activity. 5 per day! He was the first person to call me by phone. We talked about his interest in art and he started texting me photos of artwork he has completed. He inspired me to pull out my sketchbook and I sent him pictures of what I've created.

After the first three weeks, I noticed that Joel wasn't completing his assignments anymore. I made multiple attempts to contact him and finally got through. He opened up to me about his difficulties with the work. He asked me if I could teach him to read during my lunch break next year. Heartbreaking, yes, but also joyful. This is the same student who spent the first 3 months of the school year throwing materials, often messy ones, and threatening me.

My joy isn't because of his frustration. That's the heartache. But I have to feel joyful in recognizing how far Joel has come. He is finally starting to open up about his struggles and trust me enough to ask for help. I told Joel that, of course, I would find a way to help him, and that even after distance learning is over for the year, we would keep connected. I praised him for all he is doing. I'm once again reminded that behind every classroom behavior issue, there is a reason. Building classroom culture and relationships with students takes a lot of effort, but the payoff can be amazing.

In addition to the breakthroughs Joel has made, I can name so many other joyful experiences during this difficult teaching time. Most of them go back to the transformation the class made as a result of decreasing large-group instruction, providing incentives, and emphasizing the positive. I'm not going to lie. At the beginning of the year, I questioned whether I was an effective teacher for this program. During distance learning, I've been frustrated and sad, but finding joy in watching my students grow as a community and power through learning from a distance has kept me going.

It will likely be a long time before schools, and life in general, go back to "normal." For now, distance learning is what we have. So, whether I'm waving to a smiling student from my car after picking up her learning packets from the porch and dropping off treats and a book, helping a struggling student believe in himself, or just celebrating the fact that because of initial behavior issues in the classroom, I ended up teaching my students how to use technology which is now critical, I will keep trying to find the joy in teaching even from a distance.

You too can find the joy in cracked eggs and quarantine.

1. Don't give up! Each class presents new challenges. Step back from the situation and examine the issues you are having. After you do that, come up with a plan that is specifically designed for the students in front of you.
2. Emphasize the positive! Recognize students for the amazing things they do, no matter how small. Everyone needs to hear praise for their efforts and accomplishments. Dig deep if you have to. There is always something a student is doing well, even if they are disrupting your class or struggling academically. And honestly, the disrupters and strugglers need praise more than anyone.

3. Technology can be a wonderful tool in the classroom when used efficiently! If you are having difficulty keeping students engaged during whole-group learning, consider using technology to foster more individual accountability and self-paced learning. Once students are proficient in using technology, they can work independently while you conduct small-group instruction. Plus, if there is ever a need for students to learn from a distance, they will already know how to use the technology!

Writing/Thinking Exercise

If you taught during the Covid-19 crisis, list three positive interactions you had with students. If you didn't teach during that time, identify another challenging time you experienced as a teacher and list three positive interactions you had with students.

1. _____

2. _____

3. _____

Now, reflect on what you did to facilitate those positive interactions!

_____

_____

_____

Now, give yourself a pat on the back! You deserve it!

Developing Relationships with the Students: Finding Joy in the Best Part of All

Making connections with students, getting to know them as people, and guiding and supporting them as they succeed and fail academically, socially, and emotionally both in and outside of school is, in my opinion, the best and most important part of being a teacher. It's the part of teaching that will fill you up with the most joy and gratitude. It is also a key deciding factor in the experience students have in your classroom and the extent to which they succeed.

Don't get me wrong. Knowing the standards and having a firm understanding of the curriculum you are going to teach are essential in creating engaging and meaningful lessons. In addition, providing opportunities for students to make meaning of their learning through their own projects and activities gives them a sense of control and purpose, as well as helps them make higher-level connections. And of course, having well-established routines and expectations are crucial to the order and safety of your day and your students; without good management, you will have chaos on your hands and nobody will learn anything.

Everything you have read about in this book thus far about topics, kid projects and activities, and classroom management are fundamental aspects of teaching and places where joy is abundant when you let it in. But, if you don't take the time to connect with your students, to get to know them and find the genius in each of them, you will miss out on the best part of the job.

Building relationships with students can be difficult. The first obstacle is time. You are only one person and, depending on your teaching assignment, you may have as few as eight students or as many as 100. If you only have eight students, they likely have significant needs. With all of the responsibilities a teacher has, it can be challenging to find the time to talk to each student and really get to know them. Don't worry; even small, short interactions can make a big difference!

In addition to feeling crunched for time, building relationships with students can be hard simply because we are all humans. It is normal to feel at ease with some students because you have common interests and compatible personalities, while with others you feel you have nothing to connect over. Likewise, it's easy to talk to or understand certain students, while with others getting to three exchanges in a conversation is a victory. Fear not! With a little effort and practice, you and all of your students will soon be reaping the benefits of building stronger relationships in the classroom.

In this section, you'll learn how to be something that so many students need: a caring, supportive adult whom they can trust and confide in. You will read about instances in which my relationships with students compelled them to work hard and believe in themselves. And you will read about how rich a teacher's life can be when they get to know amazing people sitting in front of them for 7 hours a day. You will realize that when you build a relationship with students, not only do you provide needed support to your students, you also open yourself up to an infinite supply of joy.

Knowing You're the One they'd Tell

The first year I worked at the charter school was a tough one. I was hired to teach fourth grade. It was my fifth year as a teacher, but my first in elementary school as a general education teacher. I had been attracted to the school because of its design. The curriculum was all based in local history and science. Students got to experience learning by going on field studies, delving into primary-source documents, meeting with guest experts, and completing culminating projects. The idea that learning was an adventure meshed perfectly with my philosophy on life and teaching.

Remember in the introduction of this book when I mentioned that teaching isn't always rainbows and unicorns? Well, working at this school put me through some rough times. Don't get me wrong, there were many things I loved about the school: the curriculum, families, and commitment to creating lifelong learners to name a few.

I got to do things with kids that I probably wouldn't have at any other school. For example, one year, the entire school studied the local river. We split into cross-grade groups and each group went to a section of the river 4 times over a 2-month period. We studied the local flora and fauna of the area. Kids put on waders and collected samples of the river water, which we later examined through high-powered magnifiers attached to iPads. Kids sat and listened to nature and wrote about it. Older students helped the younger ones make their way down the trail or identify an insect they had found. Parents volunteered and weathered the days with us through heat, rain, complaining, and accidents.

Those types of experiences were what I loved about the school. But it wasn't all like that. It was a hard place to work. And it started that first year. For some reason, my co-teacher and I got off on the wrong foot. Co-teaching is like a marriage, when the partnership is strained, everyone suffers.

That year, my co-teacher and I argued about everything from where to plan to how instruction should be delivered. We had public arguments that, for me, a relatively young and sensitive teacher, were embarrassing and painful. I've since developed thicker skin, but at the time I would frequently get upset over our various arguments.

This first year also started the often-strained relationship I had with the principal. There were many wonderful things about her to be sure. She was committed to the success of the school and knew how to get things done. Many times, however, she and I just didn't see "eye to eye" and I would end up feeling unsupported and frustrated. Again, although I loved the students, the families, the curriculum, and many of my coworkers, I also had a lot of stormy times during my stay at the charter school.

So, you are probably wondering what this story is actually about. The title is "Knowing You're the One they'd Tell," and should have something to do with relationships with kids, right? Yes, I was just getting to that.

The next year, after weathering the storm in an unfamiliar grade level and a partnership that wasn't working, I switched to the K-1 loop and was paired with a teacher whom I would come to love and admire as both a teacher and a friend. We shared common beliefs about education and genuinely enjoyed working with each other. When we had disagreements, we were able to compromise and care for each other's feelings. I had the good luck and honor to teach with her for 10 years.

At the beginning of the first year my new friend and I began teaching together, a few of the parents from the previous year stopped by to visit and chat. Even though, in the area of team-teaching, the previous year had been difficult, I had still managed to make connections with the students and families.

One of the parents who stopped by had twin girls. They were excited about being in fifth grade, but a little disappointed that I hadn't looped with them. Over the summer, the parent had been talking to her girls about puberty and one of them told her mom,

"Mom, last year, my plan if I got my period at school was to go and tell Ms. Fredericks. Even though she's not my teacher anymore, that's still my plan."

I remember feeling so honored that of the two teachers and TA in the room last year, all of the other staff, including the nurse and her two new teachers and TA, she would feel most comfortable telling me something that can be embarrassing, exciting, and terrifying all at the same time. I told her mom that, of course, she should feel free to come and talk to me about anything.

Over the years, I've had kids talk to me about all kinds of things. Some of the things kids have told me are slightly funny. An embarrassed first-grader once came and whispered in my ear that she had had a "wet fart" and needed to change. I stifled my laughter, told her not to worry, and helped her find some new underwear.

Some of the things kids have told me helped me to have hope for humanity. One third-grader liked to report all of the suspicions he had that kids were bullying other kids. Some of the incidents were founded, others were not. My co-teacher and I always thanked him for taking good care of the class.

And some of the things kids have told me are really sad. One year, I noticed that a high school student in one of the consult classes I had didn't seem like herself. She told me that her mom had a late-term miscarriage over the weekend. I talked to her about it, as much as she was comfortable with, and told her to stop by my room any time she needed to.

Whenever a student opens themselves up to me, it reminds me of the great responsibility I have as a teacher. The content and the standards are important, but the relationships I build with students far exceed the urgency of any exam. I'll never forget when that mom, so many years ago, told me about her daughter's plan. Even when it's hard to be the person they'd tell, I'm glad that I am. There's joy in knowing you're the one they'd tell, because it means that you've made a connection.

You too can find joy in knowing you're the one they'd tell.

1. Make an effort to connect with students, even if you are not happy with your teaching position or you have your own troubles at home. At school, you are the person they depend on, so be dependable for those 7 hours.

2. When a student reports a classroom issue to you, listen and acknowledge that what they have to say is important. Thank them for letting you know. Whether or not you investigate the issue will depend on your judgment, but no matter what, students should feel comfortable reporting to you, because there may come a time when they report something that is very serious.

3. Let students know how and when to find you if they need you. They may never come to you; just knowing that you care may be enough for them.

Writing/Thinking Exercise

Think of a time when a student (or anyone) has confided in you about something that was bothering them. Choose a situation that didn't involve abuse, danger, or a need to report to an authority. How did you handle the situation?

What did you say?

_____

_____

What advice or sympathies did you offer?

_____

_____

What was your body language like?

_____

_____

What do you wish you had done differently?

_____

_____

Classroom Lunch

When I taught at the charter school, students and teachers ate lunch together in the classroom. The philosophy was that eating together in the classroom would foster the feeling of the class being one big happy family. It would give students and teachers a social time during the day to work on conversation skills and learn more about each other. Eating in the classroom was intended to be a more controlled environment where teachers could monitor student behavior and interactions. The sentiment behind having lunch in the classroom was admirable and seemed plausible.

In reality, it was loud, messy, and difficult. The TA had to serve the food and clean up, which made the classroom inaccessible for instruction for about 15 minutes before lunch, half an hour during lunch, and half an hour after. In addition, it was exhausting as a teacher to go without a real lunch break day in and day out. Many days, I craved a lunch in which I did not have to stop experiments involving exploding yogurt tubes or juice boxes. As much as I loved my students, I did not find joy in classroom lunch.

So, I was thrilled when I started the job at the urban high school and, by contract, was guaranteed a 40-minute, uninterrupted lunch each day. I never went to the staff lounge. I'm too introverted for that. I also never left the building to grab lunch at one of the food places close by. I'm too anxious for that, worrying that something would happen and I wouldn't make it back to class in time.

Instead, I brought my lunch in a reusable flowered lunch box every day and ate at my desk. In peace. Usually pasta, an apple, a clementine, and an energy bar. It was glorious, having my own space and time to eat. It also only took about 15 minutes, which left me nearly half an hour to play on my phone or computer or try to accomplish something. After a few weeks, I realized that, although my guaranteed 40-minute lunch was great, it was also a little boring.

So, I did not feel entirely inconvenienced when I occasionally had one or two of my students who had the same lunch period as me ask if they could eat in my room. One day, about a third of the way into the year, one of the students I had in Resource room fourth period, just never went to lunch for fifth period.

"Riannah, do you need something?" "No."

"Are you going to lunch?"

"No, I don't want to."

"Okay, well, I'm going to eat. You can stay here if you want to."

"Okay."

For the next few minutes, Riannah sat at the desk right next to mine. At first, I just carried on eating my lunch. Then, I realized that I had an opportunity in front of me. Riannah had been having a difficult year. She often skipped the Living Environment class where I was her consult teacher first period. I had numerous conversations with her grandmother about her frequent absences and failing grades. Both her grandmother and I racked our brains about ways we could support her.

When she did come to class, she often asked to go to the bathroom 20 minutes in, left, and never returned. When I told her grandmother about that creative misbehavior, she informed me that if Riannah needed to go to the bathroom, she would come to the school, escort her to the ladies' room and wait in the hall to escort her back to class. After that phone call, Riannah didn't leave to go to the bathroom in the middle of class anymore. She still skipped every few days, however, and had an average test score of approximately 37%.

I knew that she had experienced a lot of changes in the past year with her family. Her grandmother had shared with me that Riannah used to live locally when she was younger, then moved with her mom to another state 3 years ago. The summer before I had her in class, she had been visiting her dad in the city where the school was and was supposed to go back with her mom before school started up again.

A couple of days before school started, however, when other kids were enjoying last-minute camping trips and barbeques, Riannah's mom decided that Riannah was going to live with her dad and not come back with her. Basically, she abandoned her. She had a sad story and was struggling in school, and now I realized that I had been given the gift of time to spend with her.

For the rest of the lunch period, I asked Riannah about where she used to live and we Googled pictures of her little town. She told me about her school, her house, and her old friends. I'm still not sure why she stayed in my room that day, but I want to believe that our lunch period together gave her the feeling that at least one person in the school understood a little more about her situation.

Our time together wasn't a magic fix. Unfortunately, she didn't just start coming to class and passing tests. Throughout the rest of the year, I had many phone conversations and a few meetings with Riannah's grandmother, and even though she didn't succeed academically, I know that she and her family felt supported and understood when they interacted with me. And sometimes that has to be enough to bring you joy.

Another memorable lunch period I had that year was with Jolie. She was in my Resource room and we had a strong connection. According to her files, she had a rough time the previous year, but the year I had her, she was thriving. She was an extremely hard worker, organized, and responded well to the individualized support I was able to give her during Resource room.

I'd often get her assignments ahead of time so that I could preview them and highlight the teaching points, then we'd zip through them during Resource. She also really benefited from our strong connection. She liked to tell me about her baby brother and his chubby little legs and how he liked to cuddle with her in her bed. She also had a lot of emotional struggles and would write about them in a journal which she shared with me.

One day, Jolie was excited because her mom had a little extra money for food and had gotten her some instant macaroni and cheese and pizza bagels from the convenience store. She asked if she could stay in my room during her lunch period, which I also had free, and use the microwave to heat up her food. Of course, I said yes.

Although Jolie was 17 and a street-smart city kid, she was just adorable heating up her convenience store treats. She took such care to make sure she added the right amount of water to the macaroni and set the pizza bagels on the tray properly. These extra food items were so special to her because usually she ate the free lunch in the cafeteria, which was, as you might imagine, not very appetizing.

As she was getting her lunch ready, I realized how much I take for granted. Buying a few items at the convenience store would be no big deal for me, but for Jolie it was a rare occurrence. After her lunch was ready, we sat together and ate, mostly talking about her baby brother and how he could almost roll over.

Jolie, unlike Riannah, continued to flourish that year. She even made honor roll one quarter and received the Excellence Award for perseverance another quarter. My administrator told me one day that she believed that part of the reason Jolie was doing so well was because she trusted me and we had a good connection. If giving up my lunch period once in a while means that my relationship with a student helps them feel supported, then I guess I can find joy in classroom lunch after all.

You too can find joy in classroom lunch.

1. Make sure you take a break during the day. Nobody, not even a Super-Teacher can be at their best with students all day long if they don't have time to sit down for at least half an hour without being interrupted by a seven-year-old's (or any-year-old's) questions, stories, and needs.

2. Be willing to give up your break every so often if it means that you'll build a better relationship with a student. Just be sure to not give up your break every day. Find a balance that gives you the time you need and gives support to kids who need it.

3. Take an interest in your students and make sure that they know you care about their lives outside of school. Every person wants someone to share their celebrations with and confide in about their troubles. Be that someone for your students and reciprocate by sharing with them (at your comfort level) about your life outside of the classroom; it will build their trust in you and their respect for you as a real live human who has struggles and triumphs.

Writing/Thinking Exercise

Think about yourself as a child. If you could have eaten lunch one-on-one with a teacher, what would you have talked about? What would have been the most important thing you would want them to know?

_____

_____

_____

_____

_____

_____

_____

_____

An Unexpected Apology

The events in this story happened just two years ago while I was working as a Special Education consult and Resource room teacher at the urban high school. One of the classes I was assigned to as a consult teacher was an Earth Science class. The general education teacher was an energetic guy who had a passion for rocks, cared deeply about the success of his students, and was well-known among the other teachers as a goofy, caring, smart teacher. I was so grateful that he had welcomed me wholeheartedly as the consult teacher and helped me get situated as a new teacher to the school and the high school level.

At the time of this story, in May, there were 6 students in the class with special needs (LD, OHI) and 14 students who were typically developing. My job was to implement the Individual Education Plans of students with special needs, meaning that I provided assignment modifications, extra support, test accommodations, etc.

It was an integrated class, so I also worked with the students who did not have Individual Education Plans. In fact, some of the kids had no idea that I was really there to support certain people, and at times, the "typically developing" students were more needy than the children with identified special needs. Needy. Yes, that is a good word for this class!

First of all, we had a lot of turnover. From September until the end of the year, we lost 9 students from the class. Some went to different programs or schools, one ran away to another state, one got arrested, then returned and got suspended and was put on home instruction, and some just disappeared.

Of the 20 that were left on the roster, anywhere between 9 and 14 showed up daily. Of those who came, about 5 were consistently interested in passing the class. Another 3 or 4 were concerned some of the time about their success in the class, and a few came to sit on the tables or in the back and talk loudly with their friends, while Mr. G., the general education teacher, tried to teach and I tried to support those who wanted help. To top it off, it was eighth period and the kids and teachers were tired and done. Needy is the word.

In May, despite the challenges of the class, we still had to get students ready to take the end of the year state-issued exam. We knew only a few would qualify with enough lab minutes to take the exam, but we pushed on anyhow. Then one day, Mr. G. mentioned in the morning that he wasn't feeling well. By the afternoon, he was in the hospital and was out for over 2 weeks. During his absence, we all, teachers and students, missed him tremendously. The building was a little less fun, much quieter, and the kids and teachers who worked with him were definitely more stressed.

The long-term substitute assigned to the class was a retired Earth Science teacher. She was a good teacher, but the class was a mess. They behaved even more poorly and accomplished less than they had been previously. It was chaos.

One afternoon, a hall sweep was called. This meant that any students who had not made it to class on time needed to go to the cafeteria and meet with the administrator. Teachers were supposed to close and lock their doors. Hall sweeps were called often, especially towards the end of the day. This was not a new occurrence. Students should not have been surprised. There should not have been a problem. But there was.

I closed and locked the door but somehow two students, a boy and a girl who should have been hall swept managed to get in. I instructed them to go to the hall sweep. They argued with me and walked about the room. I told them they needed to leave. The girl started to comply. The boy grumbled more. Neither left. I told them once more and threatened to call security. They left. We went back to "working." I was annoyed, but not really shaken. Yet.

10 minutes later, the two students were back from the hall sweep. The girl entered relatively calmly, but the boy was visibly angry. His eyes were in a squinting position, his body was tense, and his lips were pursed as he burst into the room. He stared right at me and gave me two middle fingers. Of course, I told him he needed to leave and that I was calling security. He shouted obscenities at me and left as security got there.

I've had other kids swear at me over the years or get pissed, but this incident shook me. The boy was not typically an angry kid. He was one of the general education kids with the potential to do well if he focused. He could be moody, but he had never displayed behavior like the one he did that day.

He wasn't someone that I felt particularly connected to, but we had never had a problem before either. After he left, apparently he punched through one of the windows in the door and was suspended for 5 days. By the time he came back a week later, I had pretty much forgotten about the incident. He was back to his normal self, Mr. G. was still out, the class was more chaotic than ever, and we never discussed the incident. Until several weeks later, about 3 days before the end of the year.

Mr. G. was back and we were busy getting the 5 kids ready who had lab-qualified to take the end of the year exam. Some of the other students had asked to go to the library, including the boy from that day, and I was happily writing them passes. When I reached my hand out to give the boy his library pass, he looked right at me and addressed me, saying, "Ms. Fredericks, I'm really sorry, about that day."

All of his friends and peers were standing close by. I was so surprised that it took me a few seconds to respond. After the awkward seconds of silence, I thanked him for apologizing and validated how difficult it must have been to do so. I told him that I had been worried about him that day because it wasn't like him. He said, "Yeah, I was really mad that day." I thanked him again for apologizing and told him not to let one bad day like that take over. He nodded.

Our less than 2 minute conversation ended and he went to the library with his friends. This apology seems like a weird thing to feel joy in. It's not the apology I feel joy from. It's the fact that sometimes you don't even realize you have connections with kids. I didn't realize the boy was still thinking about the incident or felt connected enough with me to feel bad about his behavior. I had only worked with him a few times and he wasn't someone who sought out my attention or told me about his weekends, etc. It just goes to show that as a teacher, you never know how far your influence extends. That's the part of this story that gives me joy.

You too can find joy in an unexpected apology.

1. Keep your cool even when a student loses theirs. Most of the time, their anger has nothing to do with you, even if it seems directed that way.

2. If you are in a difficult situation where many students are not performing well, keep giving it your best each day. The students who want to succeed deserve your best teaching and you never know which of the other students are also benefiting from your efforts.

3. Treat every child with respect. Acknowledge to students that everyone makes mistakes and celebrate when they own up to their mistakes. We all know that is not easy to do.

Writing/Thinking Exercise

Think of a time that you behaved in a way that was angry and perhaps out of control towards another person. Examine what the other factors in your life at the time were.

_____

_____

_____

If you were to go back and have the courage to apologize, what would you say?

_____

_____

_____

How would you want to be received?

_____

_____

_____

Math Club and Scaled Representations of the Solar System

When someone asks me what my favorite subject to teach is, I always say, without hesitation, math. I love teaching math at any level. I've taught it at the Kindergarten level all the way through tutoring high school students. Usually when I profess my love for math, the person I am talking to will say something like, "Oh, math is hard" or "I never was very good at math."

I've done some reading about this phenomenon of math anxiety, and I've listened to lots of people over the years explain why they have such a hard time with math. I understand that everyone has strengths and weaknesses and that some people are more comfortable in one subject or another. The thing that baffles me is that it almost seems socially acceptable to say, "Well, I just don't get math," whereas you hardly ever hear someone say, "Well, I just don't get books." I'll get back to this point later in the story.

As a child, I was always really strong at math, but I never realized how much I loved it! When I became a teacher, gradually over the years, I realized my passion for math. I love the patterns that pop out at you. I'm not just talking about red, blue, red, blue, but patterns in the number system. Think about it, there are only 10 numbers to work with (0-9), yet if infinity could be reached, we could count to it using only those numbers! And it all happens in a pattern!

I also enjoy the way you have to sort through pieces of a puzzle to get to the answer. For example, when you try to solve a geometry problem and you have some of the angles or side lengths and you have to solve for one of the missing sides or angles. It's like a treasure hunt! You have to take each clue and use them in the right order, and eventually, you can figure out what the missing piece equals.

In math, there is almost always a "right answer." I find that very satisfying in a world that can be unpredictable. Lastly, I love the fact that once you start looking around with your "math eyes," you will see math everywhere, from the fractal patterns of tree branches to the distribution of different ethnic populations in various parts of the United States.

Over the years, as my passion for math grew and as I realized the extent of math anxiety in some kids, parents, and teachers, I started to make it part of my mission as a teacher to help people who initially claimed they "don't get math" to become more comfortable with it and eventually even love it, just a little. See how I am getting back to my earlier point?

I know I can't change the attitude that millions of people have about math, but little by little, one person at a time, I have found that I can instill a little passion for math in even the most math-phobic person. And, for kids who love math already, boy are they in for a treat when they get me for a teacher. Bring on the nerdy math conversations, projects, and impossible problems to solve!

So, you want a concrete story right? Isn't that what this book is? Yes! Let me tell you about a year that I taught third grade. I was working at the charter school. We co-taught there, but of course, since I was THE MATH PERSON and everyone knew how I loved to teach Math, I got to teach all of the math lessons.

This particular class had a strange dynamic. When we did our initial assessments at the beginning of the year, we found that there were 10 out of 34 kids performing about a year behind in Math. We also found that there were about 8 kids who were at least a year above grade level, with a few kids being even further ahead. I believe that 2 students scored like 7th graders on the standardized test. So, based on that data and the wide range of skills and abilities in Math, I realized that differentiation was going to be very important that year.

Three days of the week, for the Daily Math instruction, we had a mini-lesson that everyone attended and then we rotated the students between myself, my co-teacher, and the TA. I planned all of the parts and informed my co-teacher and TA of what each group would be working on. The groups had slightly different assignments based on their specific needs. When they came to me, the lesson was geared specifically to them.

One day of the week, I only had half of the class at a time while the other half attended PE. On that day, one group had all of the typically developing kids together and I taught them a pretty standard math skills lesson. The other group had the high-performing kids and the struggling kids. I gave the high performers projects to do along with accountability measures and sent them on their way. If the TA was there or a parent volunteer, they monitored the kids, but mostly they worked independently.

I had them do things such as make timelines of the Earth's history and indicate the amount of time that passed between each period. It was great fun for their quick-thinking brains and it gave them some independence. If they messed around, they were out of the group. Meanwhile, with the kids who struggled, I used that time to provide intense instruction in skills they had not yet mastered.

On Fridays, I did cross-curricular math with everyone. I had parent volunteers and the TA and co-teacher and we did wonderful things related to what we were studying. For example, when we studied the solar system, we figured out how much we would weigh on each planet. And as an introduction to our year as Mathematicians, we studied the oldest-known mathematical document, the Rhind papyrus. The kids and I couldn't believe that this papyrus proved that people had been doing math for at least the last 3700 years! If math had been around and important for so long, then we had better learn it!

Because of our constant immersion and celebration of math, this class, more than any other, became enamored with math. I'm talking about the high performers *and* the struggling kids! Let's start with the struggling kids. Even though we differentiated like crazy, it wasn't enough to catch everyone up, so I started a Math Club.

Once a week, the 10 kids who were below grade level stayed after school for an hour. I recruited 5 sixth-graders to stay after as well to be "tutors." Each sixth-grader was assigned 2 third-graders to work with. I taught the lessons and provided the materials, and the kids took it from there. We usually did some skill work, then activities with manipulatives, and ended with math-related games.

When word got out about Math Club and how much fun we were having, other kids wanted to join! It was heartbreaking to tell them no, but I had to keep it just for the kids who needed help. And it really worked! One little girl made two years of progress that year, according to the testing. More importantly, she gained confidence! At the beginning of the year, I would catch her copying off of other people because she was embarrassed that she didn't understand. By the end of the year, she had gained enough ground to work through problems on her own and she had grown in confidence so much that she would speak up when she didn't understand.

Another little girl, who struggled academically and had trouble with cleanliness, in the third grade ended up scoring on grade level in Math by the end of the year! One day, another student noticed how well she was doing and exclaimed, "Faith is killing it in Math!" Faith, who was shy and not used to praise from her peers, just smiled and hid behind her long, thick, chestnut brown hair.

While the kids who struggled were making good progress, so was the other end of the spectrum. One little boy, who was one of the really high performers, had an absolute passion for math. He and I became quick math comrades. When I taught the class about place value and the base ten system, Alex and I did a little side project on the Mayan counting system which was a base 20 system, but only included 3 symbols. So cool! Alex would bring in books about a math topic or connection he was interested in and we would go to town with it. He also did math projects on his own, and my favorite ever was his scaled representation of the solar system.

Alex had told me that he was working on a scaled representation of the solar system at home, so of course, I told him to bring it in and present it! After all, his work seemed like something all of the Mathematicians in the class would be excited about!

Alex was a really smart guy, but also very unorganized, slightly messy, and definitely marched to his own drum beat. He didn't care much about what others thought of him and was constantly losing things, including the shoes on his feet. That's right. This brilliant Mathematician was often walking around the classroom with one shoe on. The class, teachers, and students thought he was pretty awesome, since he was so smart and wasn't afraid to do his own thing.

We had just finished our morning meeting and were gathered for morning circle. It was the day Alex was prepared to share his scaled representation of the solar system. He went to his backpack and came back with a pile of folded and taped centimeter graph paper. He proceeded to lay it across the carpet around which we were all sitting, which was 12 feet long. He kept unfolding until the graph paper practically reached the edge of the rug.

The other 33 students and the 3 teachers just stared in amazement. It was so cool! Across the graph paper were 9 labeled dots. The first was the Sun. The last was Neptune. He scaled the distance between each planet, but not the size of the planets or the Sun. The first 4 planets were all clustered within the first 15 cm of the dot labeled "sun." For those of us more comfortable with inches, 1 inch is approximately 2.54 centimeters, so 15 centimeters is a little over 5 inches.

The first 4 planets were all within 5 inches (not even half a foot) of the Sun on this very long piece of graph paper! Next came Jupiter, which was 52 centimeters (20 inches or 1 ⅔ foot) from the Sun. Saturn was 95 centimeters (37 inches or a little over 3 feet) from the Sun. Are you getting an idea of how much farther the gas planets (Jupiter, Saturn, Uranus, Neptune) are from the Sun than the terrestrial planets (Mercury, Venus, Mars, Jupiter)? Well, listen to this... On Alex's scaled representation, Uranus was 192 centimeters (75 inches or 6 ¼ feet) and Neptune was 301 centimeters (118 inches or almost 10 feet) from the Sun!

He was so excited to explain the distances to us and show us the math he did in his notebook to figure out the scale. Most of us only understood a portion of the math he did, but to see the scale of distances laid out in front of us was something everyone could marvel at!

From the kids that struggled, like Faith, to the high achiever, like Alex, the best thing about Math that year was the support the kids gave each other and the math relationships I got to build with them. As I said earlier, that class, more than any other, developed a love of math. During the whole-group mini lessons, high-achievers often purposefully placed themselves next to friends who struggled and gently helped them along.

Throughout the year, lots of math books and projects made their way into the classroom to be shared. And at the end of the year, almost every student card I got said something about math! That year of widely diverse math learners reminds me how important it is to develop a relationship with every student so that they can achieve more than they believe is possible. That year, I found joy in celebrating every student's accomplishment, whether it was that they finally understood regrouping in subtraction or that they experimented with converting astronomical units into centimeters!

You too can find joy in Math Club and scaled representations of the solar system.

1. Be passionate about math! Even if Math wasn't your favorite subject as a student, it's part of your responsibility as a teacher to do what you can to thwart the phenomenon known as math phobia. Teach your students to love math by encouraging them to look for it in everyday places and to get excited about hard-to-solve problems.

2. Differentiate as much as possible. Yes, it may mean more planning, group-forming, and materials set up, but it's worth it. Every child deserves to be met where they are.

3. Foster a classroom community in which all learners are celebrated for their successes. Teach your students to be respectful with each other; lending a hand when they can and accepting help when necessary. Make it a place where a student is as comfortable accepting assistance from a peer as they are showing off a complex project.

Writing/Thinking Exercise

Think of a student you have who is performing above grade level. How can you inspire him/her to challenge him/herself?

_____

_____

_____

Now think of a student you have who is performing below grade level or struggling in some way. How can you inspire him/her to persevere through challenges and feel good about school?

_____

_____

_____

Misspellings

Since my teaching career included 12 years in the Kindergarten/first-grade loop, I am no stranger to misspellings. During those years, I believe that the grey matter in my head actually formed a new section which allowed me to read anything written phonetically. "Papto." Well, that says "paper towels" of course. "I wt swmng." You guessed it, that's "I went swimming." And every primary teacher knows that "Ilvu" says "I love you." To me, misspellings are wonderful because they symbolize the beginning of a child's journey as a reader and writer.

There are three misspellings that I specifically remember being touched by. The first one involved a little girl who was a struggling writer in the second grade. She was an energetic little girl with a nervous habit of pacing and jutting her head back and forth sort of like a chicken. She was very sweet, but struggled with academics and attention.

During the time I am writing about, we were learning about the seed business of the 1800s. As a part of that unit, we packaged seeds. On each packet, a student seed-factory worker wrote the name of a member of the school. When we were done, there was a package for every student and teacher in the school. Even though this little girl struggled with writing, she chose the job of labeling names.

For most of the time, a grown-up worked with her to make sure she stayed where she was supposed to be and didn't go pacing off to a different area and to ensure that she copied the names correctly from the list. As you can imagine though, with 30 other 8-year-olds working in a seed factory, there was a lot going on, and at times, she had to work on her own.

She worked very hard that day and was extremely focused on the task. Hands-on activities were engaging for her and often worked out better than straight academics. She wrote my name (Ms. Fredericks) on a seed packet and was so excited to deliver it to me. I looked at it and smiled to myself. I didn't have the heart to tell her that it said Ms. Frog! I just gave her a hug and professed my thanks to no end. That moment helped me feel the joy of the special bond teachers and students develop.

The next misspelling is a really "good" one. When I was teaching first grade one year, we were studying jobs of the 1800s. The students had been to visit the local outdoor museum that depicted a village from the 1800s. They had read many books on occupations from long ago. For our final project, each student was to become a worker from the 1800s and we were going to create a village in the auditorium for the families to come see.

We had blacksmiths, tinsmiths, wheelwrights, doctors, apothecaries, coopers, and so on. For one of the writing projects, students had to create an advertisement about their job so the other villagers would be persuaded to come to them.

One of the little boys who was going to portray a doctor came to me with his writing so I could give him some feedback. He had drawn a very handsome person with a stethoscope and a big smile on his face and oval-shaped ears that kids like to add to their drawings of people. I complimented all of the details in his drawing and told him to go back and write some words.

He skipped back to his seat and copied the word "Doctor" from the word wall and then came back to show it to me. I complimented his fine handwriting and spelling and then asked him,

"So, if there were other doctors in the village, what would make people want to come see you?"

He kind of stared at me.

I said, "What makes you the best doctor?"

Then he looked at me with his big hazel eyes and said, "Well, I am good!"

I said, "Oh, well, you should write that down!"

So, off he went back to his seat, and in a few minutes, he was back with his paper, which said:

"Doctor.

I m god."

I said, "Well this is very convincing! I'm sure people would want to come to you!"

We fixed the spelling another day and added more about what made him a GOOD doctor, but in that moment, I sure did feel the joy of teaching a student to write!

The third misspelling that was special to me came from a Kindergartener in the form of a Christmas gift. This little girl had what I like to call a "strong personality." She would often test the limits. For example, she might insist that she had to go to the bathroom just as we were getting ready to go outside. Or she would take a really long time to finish an assignment and still be "working" long after we had all moved on to the next activity. One time, she "forgot" to come out for recess. That evoked a moment of panic in my co-teacher and me. She also had some troubling behaviors such as lying or taking things that didn't belong to her.

Through these behaviors, though, I could see a smart little girl who was a leader, and who had the potential to do great things. She was articulate, caught on easily to new concepts, and was already starting to read at the beginning of Kindergarten. I remember when my co-teacher and I met with her parents for the first parent-teacher conference in October.

At the start of the conference, they were both quiet and sitting sort of hunched over. I think they were nervous about what we were going to say because they knew their child well and she displayed the same types of behaviors at home. When I said, "Kristen has a strong personality" and we went on to tell them about how her behavior had positive aspects, they both seemed to breathe a sigh of relief. The dad said to me, "That's the most positive way anyone has described Kristen!"

The dad may have just thought I was being nice, but the thing is, I meant it. I really loved Kristen's "strong personality." She and I got along great, even through her ups and downs. Slowly, by connecting with her, having conversations with her, and giving her responsibility, she started to misbehave less. In fact, she turned out to be a good helper to some of the other students who struggled, especially in Math. She would help them count or sort their objects or complete whatever task was assigned.

At Christmas time, she gave me a square 4-inch canvas with some equations written, a kindergarten person drawn, some sparkly jewels glued on, and the sentence, "I lick Math becus it maks sens." It's one of my favorite gifts ever! I still have it and Kristen is now in the 7th grade.

I had the good fortune to have Kristen in my class again two years later when I taught third grade. Her dad still mentioned that first conference we had and how he had never heard Kristen's personality described in such a positive way. And, Kristen still had that "strong personality," which she had put to good use.

Without being asked, she would often sit next to friends who struggled with assignments and help them. She was a gifted teacher. As an eight-year-old, she understood how to show someone how to do something rather than do it for them. She was patient when someone was confused and would say it or show it in a different way.

She still had behaviors that were not so positive. For example, she would break out into a maniacal, loud laugh and interrupt the class if something remotely funny happened. Then, of course, the rest of the class would get off task.

Still, her positives far outweighed those irritating behaviors. She was a good friend who stood up for kids who were being bullied. She was an amazing teacher and a hard worker herself. Her canvas about "licking math" helps me feel the joy of finding the good in kids, reassuring parents, and inspiring students to love learning.

You too can find joy in misspellings.

1. Be respectful and positive, but truthful with parents. Every parent needs to hear about the amazing parts of their child. They also need honest feedback about any struggles their child may have and how they can best support them.
2. Celebrate emerging writers and anyone else who is learning something new. Teach students to "do the best they can and then move on." Students need to feel uninhibited by their mistakes and imperfections in order to take risks in their writing and other learning.
3. Find the good in each child. There may be some outwardly annoying and irritating characteristics of a certain child, but deep down there are gifts and genius in everyone. Find the good in a child and he or she will thrive in the classroom and in life.

Writing/Thinking Exercise

Think of a "challenging" student you have in your class now or have taught in the past. List at least three positive attributes about the child that you could tell his/her parents.

1. _____

2. _____

3. _____

4. _____

5. _____

6. _____

Seeing Kids Again after You Are Technically Done with Them

Teaching is such a strange profession. If you teach in a traditional setting, for 10 months, you spend more of your waking hours with a group of other people's children each day than you do with your own family. You shed literal blood, sweat, and tears to accomplish the task of giving your students the best possible opportunities academically, artistically, socially, and emotionally.

By the end of the year, you and your students know each other so well that you are practically family. And then, the magical day comes. Backpacks are cast aside, poems about pencils and unfriendly teachers' faces are recited, and a year's worth of work is burned, trashed, or merely forgotten.

The day I'm referring to is the last day of school of course. After roughly 75,600 minutes, you are technically done with them. But then, sooner or later, you bump into at least some of them in halls, they come back to visit, or you run into them in public. It's inevitable. And that is what this story is all about.

The place I usually see kids after I'm technically done with them is back at school of course. When the new year begins, I am always blessed with many visitors. When I co-taught at the charter school, our Open House was held before school began and was a chance for students and families to come in, check out the classroom, and meet the teacher.

Every year, several of our old students from various years would pop in for visits. It was always great to see them after a long summer of absence making my heart grow fonder of them. Let's face it, by the end of the year, I was tired of many of them. But after 10 weeks of separation, my love for them came back; especially since I knew someone else would be in charge of them from now on! They also looked 3 inches taller after the summer break and sounded 2 years more mature and articulate.

At the high school level, I love seeing kids in the hall the following year. Some of them barely nod their heads to acknowledge me as we pass each other, while others shout my name down the crowded hallway or high five me. This year, one boy figured out where my new classroom was, popped in, and asked me if I had any candy! When he was in my class, we did Friday candy. Here he was, not in my class anymore, visiting on a Tuesday, asking for candy! I gave him a few pieces of course.

The best place to see kids after I'm technically done with them is in public. Not all meet-ups are joyful for the kids. Once I ran into a past student at the grocery store who looked like he wanted to melt into the floor during the 5-minute conversation I had with his mom. Another time, I saw two of my old students playing outside when I was running through their neighborhood, and instead of saying hi to me, they ran in the opposite direction down the street!

Most of the time, seeing my students years later at a random place is wonderful. I've run into past students everywhere from the grocery store (sometimes shopping, sometimes working!) to the local theater (either enjoying the show or acting in it!). I've even seen kids at local running races.

One time, I "ran" into one of my old Kindergarten students who was now twelve years old volunteering at a 5K giving out water at the end. He was so excited when he saw me finish that he ran up to me and hugged me, nearly knocking me over, shouting, "You did it, Ms. F.! Great job." Then he tossed a bottle of water at me! I've had so many meet-ups over the years, but one of my favorites happened at a local park about four years ago.

The story goes like this: I was out for a leisurely hike with my daughters and mom at a local park. We had just parked the car and were walking down to where the trail began. All of a sudden, my mom asked, "Why is that young man running after you?" I looked back to see a tall, blond 20ish-year-old who had parked his car in a rush and was running after me. Strange.

Then I heard him calling "Ms. Fredericks, Ms. Fredericks!" I stopped walking and waited for him to catch up to me. By this point, I had realized that this grown man was most likely a past student of mine. As he came up to me, panting and out of breath, he excitedly explained that he had seen me walking and just had to stop his car so he could say hi.

I looked very carefully at his face and recognized him as a young boy I had in my first-grade class 15 years prior. He was the young blond boy who often got lost in his own thoughts and had to be redirected to mentally join the class. He was also the student whose parents got an uncomfortable call home about him using a pencil to poke his friend in the behind.

Now he is a grown-up studying astronomy in college. He is well-spoken, physically fit, and thrilled to have spotted his old first-grade teacher walking down the street. I'm sure he does not remember most of the content knowledge he learned in first grade. I don't remember much of the information we learned that year either, but luckily academic content is not the most important part of schooling.

I am thankful that he remembers I was his teacher and went out of his way to greet me 15 years later. I hope that he remembers starting our days with song, the field trip to search for fossils, the class-written play we put on for families about settler life, and the lessons we had, explicit and organic, about how to be a good friend and human being.

I hope that somehow, in some way, being part of my first-grade class taught him to be a curious learner and a quality human being. I hope the same is true for all kids I've had the honor to teach over the past 20 years, because if it is, then I know I can find the joy in teaching no matter what the obstacles are.

You too can find joy in seeing kids again after you are technically done with them.

1. Welcome past students into your class (at the appropriate times of course). If a student pops in to say hi or ask you something, take the time to talk with them and help them if needed. As I've said before, building relationships is possibly the best and most important part of teaching.

2. If you have been teaching for a while and you live in the same area as your students, expect that you may see them in public. I've made the mistake of wearing pajama pants to the grocery store only to run into one of my old students. Being a teacher can be like being a celebrity. The paparazzi may be watching! Be presentable and be a model citizen.

3. This one is really important. When you run into a student, and it is years later and you cannot figure out who they are right away, take a moment, and really look at their face. Chances are, as you are looking, they will say something about the class they were in and the year and you will suddenly see their younger face and figure out who they are. I've done this many times and it has always worked.

Writing/Thinking Exercise

Imagine that you see one of your students in the community 10 years from now. List the most important things you want them to remember about being in your class and having you as a teacher.

1. _____

2. _____

3. _____

4. _____

5. _____

Final Thoughts:
Spread the Joy

I chose to end this book with the story "Seeing Kids Again after You Are Technically Done with Them," because it illustrates the responsibility and influence teachers have. At first, I thought I was writing this book to help teachers learn to live happy, long lives as educators. And that is one very important impact that I hope this book has on readers.

Now I realize that finding the joy benefits everyone that a teacher comes in contact with. A joyful teacher spreads that positivity to students, families, and colleagues, creates better and more creative lessons, and doesn't give up despite obstacles that plague his or her classroom, school, district, state, or country.

Simply put, a joyful teacher is a better teacher. A better teacher not only focuses on making sure that students learn content and get good grades, but ensures that the classroom is a place that fosters the development of human beings who are curious learners, persevere when things are hard, feel cared for, and learn to treat others kindly; a place where students find the joy in learning.

Every day as a teacher, I remind myself that my influence as an educator, my ability to find and spread joy, can last much longer than 10 months. For as long as I remain in teaching, I will strive to be a joyful, better teacher because

I want to contribute as much as possible to a positive life for students in the present and future.

I know that not all of the students I teach will succeed. Sadly, I have had students who, in their young adult lives, have landed in jail, fought mental illness, or passed away. We don't have the power to ensure that each child we teach is prosperous, but we can do our best to give them the richest possible learning experiences, and be models of kind, caring citizens.

This combination will lead to the greatest possibility for a lifelong positive memory of their time with us. So, whether you are wading through toilet water or trying to understand a young scientist describe his scaled model of the great beyond, remember, what you do matters. Find the joy in each crazy moment and project it, because you never know how powerful and long-lasting your influence on a child may be. When you find that joy, spread it by telling others your stories! I, for one, can't wait to hear them.

Thank You

Teaching and writing a book are alike in one important way; neither can be accomplished well as a solitary pursuit. Thank you to my family and friends for supporting me through the long process of writing this book. Thank you also to the co-workers I have been blessed to teach with side-by-side over the years. I couldn't teach or write well without all of you in my life.

Made in the USA
Middletown, DE
22 February 2022

61662908R00096